DAILY DEVOTIONAL

PEACE

IN THE MIDST OF IT ALL

365 DAYS

CECILYN J. WASHINGTON
WITH SHARON THOMAS

WestBow Press books may be ordered through booksellers or by contacting:

WestBow Press
A Division of Thomas Nelson & Zondervan
1663 Liberty Drive
Bloomington, IN 47403
www.westbowpress.com
1 (866) 928-1240

ISBN: 978-1-9736-8283-7 (sc)
ISBN: 978-1-9736-9203-4 (hc)
ISBN: 978-1-9736-8284-4 (e)

Library of Congress Control Number: 2019921134

Printed in China.

WestBow Press rev. date: 07/20/2020

WESTBOW
P R E S S®
A DIVISION OF THOMAS NELSON
& ZONDERVAN

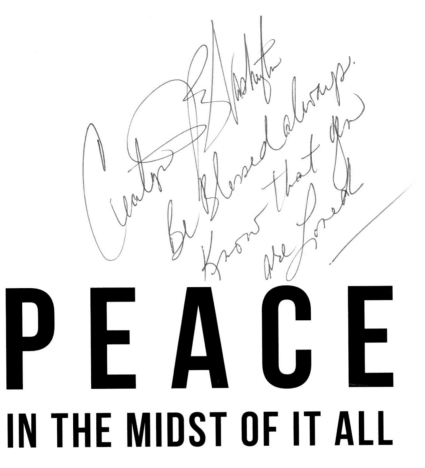

PEACE

IN THE MIDST OF IT ALL

January 1

The Father - Blessed be God, even the Father of our Lord Jesus Christ, the Father of mercies, and the God of all comfort; 2 Corinthians 1:3 KJV

Abba Father!!

January 2

Peace - Now the Lord of peace himself give you peace always by all means. The Lord be with you all. 2 Thessalonians 3:16 KJV

The Lord of Peace will always be available to you, at all times. Peace does not come easy; you have to seek after it. Seek peace, you will find it.

January 3

Peace - They must turn from evil and do good; they must seek peace and pursue it. 1 Peter 3:11 NIV

Avoid disharmony - I will seek peace and receive my blessings.

January 4

Fast And Pray - And when they had fasted and prayed, and laid their hands on them, they sent them away. Acts 13:3 KJV

Fasting and praying is a way to fellowship with God without food. Going without food is emptying yourself to focus yourself to rely on God to fill you with His strength and wisdom to move forward. You can fast and pray as an individual or as a group.

January 5

Great Are His Mercies - For as the heavens are high above the earth, So great is His mercy toward those who fear Him; Psalm 103:11 NKJV

We cannot imagine the meaning of "So great" any more than we can measure the distance from earth to heaven. But God's mercies are "So great", toward those with Godly fear.

January 6

Walk - When Abram was ninety-nine years old, the LORD appeared to Abram and said to him, "I am almighty God; walk before Me and be blameless. And I will make My covenant between Me and you, and will multiply you exceedingly." Genesis 17:1-2 NKJV

The covenant with Abram was extended to me. Help me LORD to be blameless as I walk before You.

January 7

Praise The Lord - Let everything that has breath praise the LORD. Praise the LORD! Psalm 150:6 NKJV

All of God's living creatures should give admiration unto the LORD.

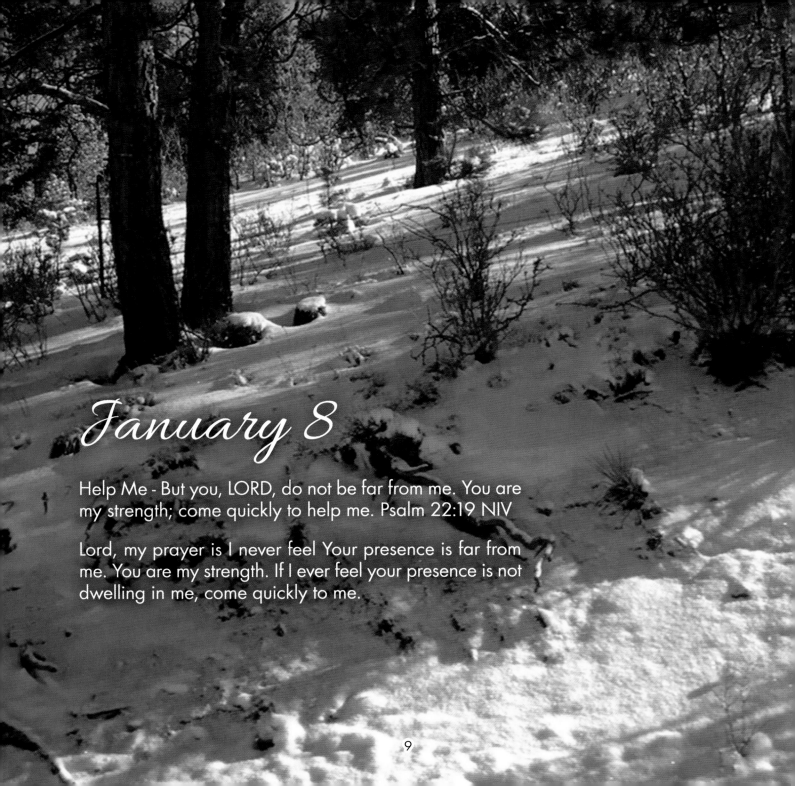

January 8

Help Me - But you, LORD, do not be far from me. You are my strength; come quickly to help me. Psalm 22:19 NIV

Lord, my prayer is I never feel Your presence is far from me. You are my strength. If I ever feel your presence is not dwelling in me, come quickly to me.

January 9

Salvation - The LORD is my strength and song, and is become my salvation.
Psalm 118:14 KJV

I will sing praises unto the LORD, the LORD is the giver of my strength, the LORD has saved my soul from sin. When I turned to Him, He began to be my salvation.

January 10

Hope - For we are saved by hope: but hope that is seen is not hope: for what a man seeth, why doth he yet hope for? But if we hope for that we see not, then do we with patience wait for it. Romans 8:24-25 KJV

I am confident that my expected end will be living forevermore with my Lord and Savior.

January 11

Sustain - Cast thy burden upon the LORD, and he shall sustain thee: he shall never suffer the righteous to be moved. Psalm 55:22 KJV

The LORD can bear the weight of my burdens. I freely give my burdens to the LORD. The LORD will take my burdens and hold me up.

January 12

Life Up A Standard - So shall they fear the name of the LORD from the west, and glory from the rising of the sun. When the enemy shall come in like a flood, the Spirit of the LORD shall lift up a standard against him. Isaiah 59:19 KJV

There are times when we seem to be singled out for special events in your life. Just as the pressure from a flood can be overwhelming so can the pressures of life or special events in your life seem overwhelming. Although the pressures against me can be strong, God has given me the Spirit of the LORD, which is stronger.

January 13

Walk - And he blessed Joseph, and said, God, before whom my fathers Abraham and Isaac did walk, the God which fed me all my life long unto this day, Genesis 48:15 KJV

My God is the God of Abraham, Isaac, and Jacob. God will walk with me all my days.

January 14

Compassion - The LORD is gracious and righteous;
our God is full of compassion. Psalm 116:5 NIV

15

God is faithful and His mercies endureth forevermore.

January 15

My Heart - Your word I have hidden in my heart, That I might not sin against You. Psalm 119:11 NKJV

The Holy Spirit brings to our remembrance the Word of God that we have in our hearts and minds. He can only bring into remembrance what is within us.

January 16

Wait On The Lord - Wait on the LORD; Be of good courage, And He shall strengthen your heart; Wait, I say, on the LORD! Psalm 27:14 NKJV

The LORD will strengthen my heart, so I will be of good courage, as I wait on Him.

January 17

My Burden Is Light - Come unto me, all ye that labour and are heavy laden, and I will give you rest. Take my yoke upon you, and learn of me; for I am meek and lowly in heart: and ye shall find rest unto your souls. For my yoke is easy, and my burden is light. Matthew 11:28-30 KJV

We have an open invitation to go to the Lord. We just need to accept the invitation and go. He has promised to take our burdens and give us rest, rest that only He can give. Rest for your soul is waiting for you.

January 18

Mercy For Ever - To him that made great lights: for his mercy endureth for ever: The sun to rule by day: for his mercy endureth for ever: Psalm 136:7-8 KJV

To Him who made all things, His mercy endureth for ever.

January 19

Liberty - All things are lawful for me, but all things are not helpful. All things are lawful for me, but I will not be brought under the power of any. 1 Corinthians 6:12 NKJV

I can do anything I please, but I ask the question, does it glorify God? Am I willing to reap the consequences of what I have sown? I will strive to live so that nothing or no one will have power over me.

January 20

Walk - Then said the LORD unto Moses, Behold, I will rain bread from heaven for you; and the people shall go out and gather a certain rate every day, that I may prove them, whether they will walk in my law, or no. Exodus 16:4 KJV

This was a Divine supply of food for their daily needs. They were only to gather what was needed for the day and trust that God would provide for them again tomorrow. Are you trusting God on your daily walk?

January 21

Speak No Evil - Set a guard, O LORD, over my mouth; Keep watch over the door of my lips. Psalm 141:3 NKJV

You say in Your Word, "Out of the same mouth come praise and cursing. My brothers and sisters this should not be." James 3:10 NIV. Help me O LORD with my communications.

January 22

Remember Me - Remember me, O LORD, with the favor You have toward Your people. Oh, visit me with Your salvation, Psalm 106:4 NKJV

Think on me LORD with your favor, for I know there is no salvation apart from You.

January 23

According To The Flesh - Those who live according to the flesh have their minds set on what the flesh desires; but those who live in accordance with the Spirit have their minds set on what the Spirit desires. Romans 8:5 NIV

To live my life according to the flesh leads to my demise to live according to the Spirit leads to life and peace.

January 24

Blessed - "But blessed is the one who trusts in the LORD, whose confidence is in him. They will be like a tree planted by the water that sends out its roots by the stream. It does not fear when heat comes; its leaves are always green. It has no worries in a year of drought and never fails to bear fruit." Jeremiah 17:7-8 NIV

I am blessed!! My confidence and trust are in the Lord. My roots are planted deep in the Lord and I have given Him my worries. I will SHOUT, "I shall not be moved"!!

January 25

Wait On The Lord - The LORD is good unto them that wait for him, to the soul that seeketh him. It is good that a man should both hope and quietly wait for the salvation of the LORD. Lamentations 3:25-26 KJV

As I seek the LORD with my whole heart it teaches me to wait on Him with the hope that is within me.

January 26

Humble Yourself - Humble yourselves, therefore, under God's mighty hand, that he may lift you up in due time. 1 Peter 5:6 NIV

Help me to be humble to do Your will. I will be lifted up on this side of heaven or on the other side.

January 27

Walk - And you shall teach them the statues and the laws, and show them the way in which they must walk and the work they must do. Exodus 18:20 NKJV

Are you a walking example of a Christian? Do your works show your love for God and mankind?

January 28

Teach me - Accept, LORD, the willing praise of my mouth, and teach me your laws.
Psalm 119:108 NIV

I lift my voice in praise for who You are, teach me your Word.

January 29

You Are Chosen - You whom I have taken from the ends of the earth, And called from its farthest regions, And said to you, 'You are My servant, I have chosen you and have not cast you away: Isaiah 41:9 NKJV

I am a believer in Jesus Christ. All believers have been taken from the ends of the earth, called and chosen by God to be a servant. Because of His grace, I was not cast away.

January 30

Seek My Face - Hear, O LORD, when I cry with my voice! Have mercy also upon me, and answer me. When You said, "Seek My face," My heart said to You, "Your face, LORD, I will seek." Psalm 27:7-8 NKJV

The Lord will hear my voice when I cry out and have mercy on me, and answer me!!

January 31

Strength - In the day when I cried out, You answered me, And made me bold with strength in my soul. Psalm 138:3 NKJV

God can give you a quick answer that will strengthen your soul.

February 1

Love - Love does no harm to a neighbor; therefore love is the fulfillment of the law. Romans 13:10 NKJV

Love your neighbor as you love yourself. Do I love my
neighbor? If no, today is a good day to start trying.
Who is your neighbor? Read Luke 10:25-37.

February 2

Fault - Confess your faults one to another, and pray one for another, that ye may be healed. The effectual fervent prayer of a righteous man availeth much. James 5:16 KJV

I need to be in a close relationship with other believers so I can share my strongholds. The prayer of a righteous person is powerful and effective because God hears and takes actions. Prayer changes things.

February 3

Walk - I will walk among you and be your God, and you will be my people.
Leviticus 26:12 NIV

We are God's chosen people. He walks with us daily as we go through life's journey. Through the good times and the bad times.

February 4

Work - And whatsoever ye do, do it heartily, as to the Lord, and not unto men; Colossians 3:23 KJV

Whatever I do in word or deed, I will do it unto the Lord and not unto men. I will do what is pleasing to the Lord and not to man.

February 5

God Of Peace And Love - Finally, brothers and sisters, rejoice! Strive for full restoration, encourage one another, be of one mind, live in peace. And the God of love and peace will be with you. 2 Corinthians 13:11 NIV

I want to start today by seeking someone that I can encourage and end with God's peace and love. I want to know I didn't tear down but lifted up. Be mindful to begin at home.

February 6

Purpose - But you are a chosen people, a royal priesthood, a holy nation, God's special possession, that you may declare the praises of him who called you out of darkness into his wonderful light. 1 Peter 2:9 NIV

I need to know my identity and my purpose. I have been called out of the darkness into the marvelous light to proclaim the praise of the One that has chosen me.

February 7

Peace - But the meek shall inherit the earth; and shall delight themselves in the abundance of peace. Psalm 37:11 KJV

The meek do not seek after inheritance. The inheritance seeks after them and they will have Peace.

February 8

Fear Not - Fear not, for I am with you;
Be not dismayed, for I am your God I
will strengthen you, Yes, I will help you,
I will uphold you with My righteous right
hand.' Isaiah 41:10 NKJV

God, my protector, is faithful and will give
me the strength to bear all of my trials.

February 9

Boast - This is what the LORD says: "Let not the wise boast of their wisdom or the strong boast of their strength or the rich boast of their riches, but let the one who boasts boast about this: that they have the understanding to know me, that I am the LORD, who exercises kindness, justice and righteousness on earth, for in these I delight," declares the LORD. Jeremiah 9:23-24 NIV

My boasting should be of the LORD and not of myself.

February 10

Walk - Yea, though I walk through the valley of the shadow of death, I will fear no evil: for thou art with me; thy rod and thy staff they comfort me. Psalm 23:4 KJV

As I journey through this land, I will fear no evil. I know God will guide and protect me and this gives me comfort as I walk through this barren land.

February 11

He First Loved Us - There is no fear in love; but perfect love casts out fear, because fear involves torment. But he who fears has not been made perfect in love. We love Him because He first loved us. 1 John 4:18-19 NKJV

God has not given us a spirt of fear. God is love and there is no fear in love. He died to show His love for me, knowing that I am not worthy but He sees value in me. His love has no limits.

February 12

A Friend - A friend loves at all time, and a brother is born for a time of adversity. Proverbs 17:17 NIV

True friends strengthen each other in the Lord. A brother or sister in Christ is there during difficult times. Are you a true friend and a brother or sister in Christ?

February 13

Love - Let love be without dissimulation. Abhor that which is evil; cleave to that which is good. Be kindly affectioned one to another with brotherly love; in honour preferring one another; Romans 12:9-10 KJV

Beginning in the home, show brotherly love. Behave like a Christian by being Christ-like. Show sincere love from the heart.

February 14

God Is Love - And we have known and believed the love that God has for us. God is love, and he who abides in love abides in God, and God in him. 1 John 4:16 NKJV

God is love. We should show the love of God within us by loving our fellow man.

February 15

Love - And now abide faith, hope, love, these three; but the greatest of these is love. 1 Corinthians 13:13 NKJV

Love is the greatest of these because God is love. Show love today!!

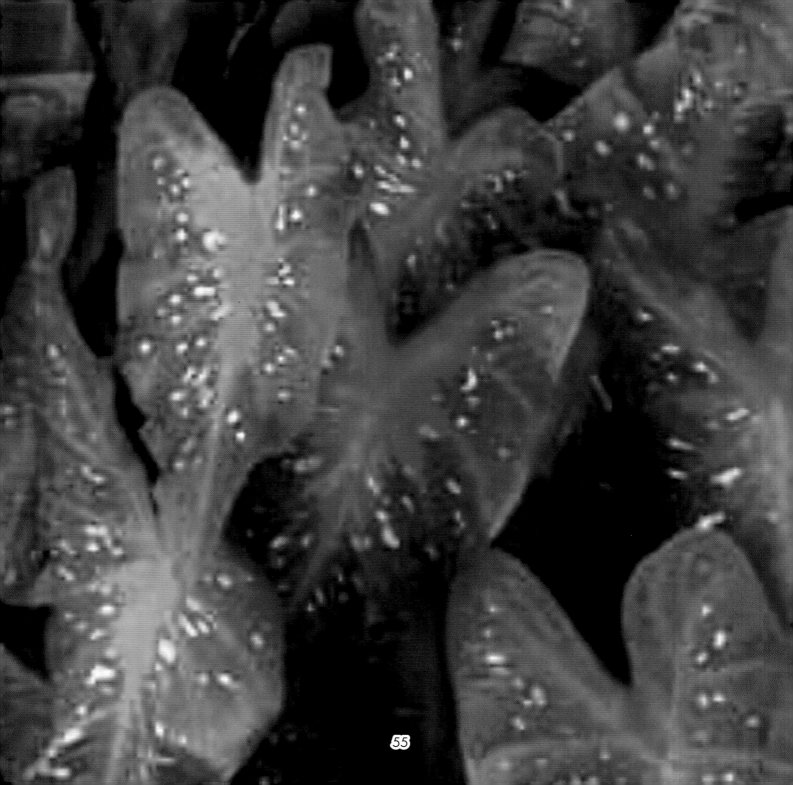

February 16

True Worshipers - But the hour is coming, and now is, when the true worshipers will worship the Father in spirit and truth; for the Father is seeking such to worship Him. John 4:23 NKJV

True worship is praise and thanksgiving knowing and appreciating God's mercy toward me.

February 17

Walk - But as for me, I will walk in my integrity; Redeem me and be merciful to me. Psalm 26:11 NKJV

When you are found doing the right thing in all circumstances and being true to yourself, people will notice your walk.

February 18

Beloved - Beloved, let us love one another, for love is of God; and everyone who loves is born of God and knows God. 1 John 4:7 NKJV

Beloved, let us love one another as we love God. Is there someone in my life that I do not love? God help me to show Godly love to everyone.

February 19

Love - And this commandment have we from him, That he who loveth God love his brother also. 1 John 4:21 KJV

The command has been given. So, I ask myself, am I loving my brother with the same amount of love I show God? Do I need to take an inventory of my love walk?

February 20

Strength And Shield - The LORD is my strength and my shield; my heart trusted in him, and I am helped: therefore my heart greatly rejoiceth; and with my song will I praise him. Psalm 28:7 KJV

The praises of the LORD will always be in my mouth. I will lift my hands and give Him praise. With Him by my side, I am protected and strong.

February 21

Life And Peace - For to be carnally minded is death; but to be spiritually minded is life and peace. Romans 8:6 KJV

I will keep my mind on Spiritual things to have an endless life and peace with God. I will not satisfy my flesh and live apart from God.

February 22

Life And Peace - The mind governed by the flesh is death, but the mind governed by the Spirit is life and peace. Romans 8:6 NIV

The actions that my flesh desires can lead to death, so I will choose to be led by the Spirit that I may have life eternal and peace.

February 23

Peace Of God - And the peace of God, which passeth all understanding, shall keep your hearts and minds through Christ Jesus. Philippians 4:7 KJV

The peace of God is unexplainable. But what a joy to experience!! God's peace will guard my hearts and minds as I encounter life's trials and tribulations.

February 24

Walk - For You have delivered my soul from death. Have You not kept my feet from falling, That I may walk before God In the light of the living? Psalm 56:13 NKJV

As I walk among the living before God and mankind, I will show my gratefulness for my deliverance.

February 25

Healed Me - O LORD my God, I cried out to You, And You healed me. Psalm 30:2 NKJV

In my time of need, I cried out to You and You healed me.

February 26

Love - Above all, love each other deeply, because love covers over a multitude of sins.
1 Peter 4:8 NIV

Love forgives. Love keeps no record of wrong. Love will make you confront the sinner, but hide the sin from others.

February 27

Love - Beloved, if God so loved us, we ought also to love one another. 1 John 4:11 KJV

Help me to always be mindful of the love God has for me, so that I may show that love to others.

February 28

Saved By Grace - But because of his great love for us, God, who is rich in mercy, made us alive with Christ even when we were dead in transgressions - it is by grace you have been saved. Ephesians 2:4-5 NIV

We are saved by grace. We have not done anything to receive this grace. We are dead in our sins when we are separated from God.

February 29

Presence - You make known to me the path of life; you will fill me with joy in your presence, with eternal pleasures at your right hand. Psalm 16:11 NIV

God will show me my path through His word. God will bring my body and soul through this life and through death to full and everlasting pleasure.

March 1

Success - Commit to the LORD whatever you do,
and he will establish your plans. Proverbs 16:3 NIV

My plans should never be made without God. My plans need to align with God's plan. If I put God's work first and do what He wants, He will provide me with what I need.

March 2

Walk - For the LORD God is a sun and shield: the LORD will give grace and glory: no good thing will he withhold from them that walk uprightly. Psalm 84:11 KJV

The LORD God is a great light and protector. He is working everything in my life for my good. Help me to walk uprightly.

March 3

Favor - May the favor of the Lord our God rest on us; establish the work of our hands for us - yes, establish the work of our hands. Psalm 90:17 NIV

I know that my work in the Lord is not in vain. I want to leave a legacy.

March 4

Love Of God - In this the love of God was manifested toward us, that God has sent His only begotten Son into the world, that we might live through Him. 1 John 4:9 NKJV

Jesus was not only sent to this world as a sacrifice for our sins but to give us an example of a Christian's walk.

March 5

Make A Joyful Noise - O come, let us sing unto the LORD: let us make a joyful noise to the rock of our salvation. Psalm 95:1 KJV

Join me in praising the LORD. Shout hallelujah to the Rock of our salvation!!

March 6

Make A Joyful Noise - Let us come before his presence with thanksgiving, and make a joyful noise unto him with psalms. Psalm 95:2 KJV

Join me in praising the LORD. As we come together before His presence, let us give thanks and praise for who He is.

81

March 7

Knowledge - The fear of the LORD is the beginning of knowledge: but fools despise wisdom and instruction. Proverbs 1:7 KJV

A good understanding comes to those who exercise reverencing the LORD.

March 8

The Almighty - "I am the Alpha and the Omega, the Beginning and the End, " says the Lord, "who is and who was and who is to come, the Almighty." Revelation 1:8 NKJV

He is God - yesterday, today and tomorrow. He is the great I AM!!

March 9

Walk - I will walk before the LORD in the land of the living. Psalm 116:9 KJV

My walk before man is showing my love for the LORD.

March 10

Laughter - All the days of the oppressed are wretched, but the cheerful heart has a continual feast. Proverbs 15:15 NIV

It's all in the state of the heart. We cannot choose our circumstances, but we can choose our attitude in our circumstances.

March 11

Blessed - Blessed are the pure in heart: for they shall see God. Matthew 5:8 KJV

Lord purify my heart.

March 12

Praise You - I will praise You, O LORD, with my whole heart; I will tell of all Your marvelous works. Psalm 9:1 NKJV

As I think on Your marvelous works, there is praise on my lips. I lift my hands and praise You for who You are. I will tell of Your goodness when the opportunity is presented. Help me to be bold in presenting the gospel.

March 13

God Of Peace - May God himself, the God of peace, sanctify you through and through. May your whole spirit, soul and body be kept blameless at the coming of our Lord Jesus Christ. 1 Thessalonians 5:23 NIV

I am not who I used to be. God will complete the process He has started within my mind, body, and spirit. And I will be presented blameless at His coming.

March 14

Comfort - Blessed be God, even the Father of our Lord Jesus Christ, the Father of mercies, and the God of all comfort; Who comforteth us in all our tribulation, that we may be able to comfort them which are in any trouble, by the comfort wherewith we ourselves are comforted of God. 2 Corinthians 1:3-4 KJV

I have within me the compassion to comfort someone in need with the same comfort I receive from my God of comfort.

March 15

Things Not Seen - While we look not at the things which are seen, but at the things which are not seen: for the things which are seen are temporal; but the things which are not seen are eternal. 2 Corinthians 4:18 KJV

The things you can see here on earth are temporary. Through faith, set your eyes on heavenly things you cannot see, for these things are eternal.

March 16

Walk - I will walk about in freedom, for I have sought out your precepts. Psalm 119:45 NIV

I will seek Your instructions and walk in freedom.

March 17

In My Distress - In my distress I called upon the LORD, and cried to my God: and he did hear my voice out of his temple, and my cry did enter into his ears. 2 Samuel 22:7 KJV

In my distress, I called out to the Lord and His ears heard my cry. When you are suffering, talk to the Lord.

March 18

Owe No Man - Owe no man any thing but to love one another: for he that loveth another hath fulfilled the law. Romans 13:8 KJV

You will have debt(s), but you need to be faithful in paying your debt(s) off. The debt of love is continuous, it is a debt that will never be paid off.

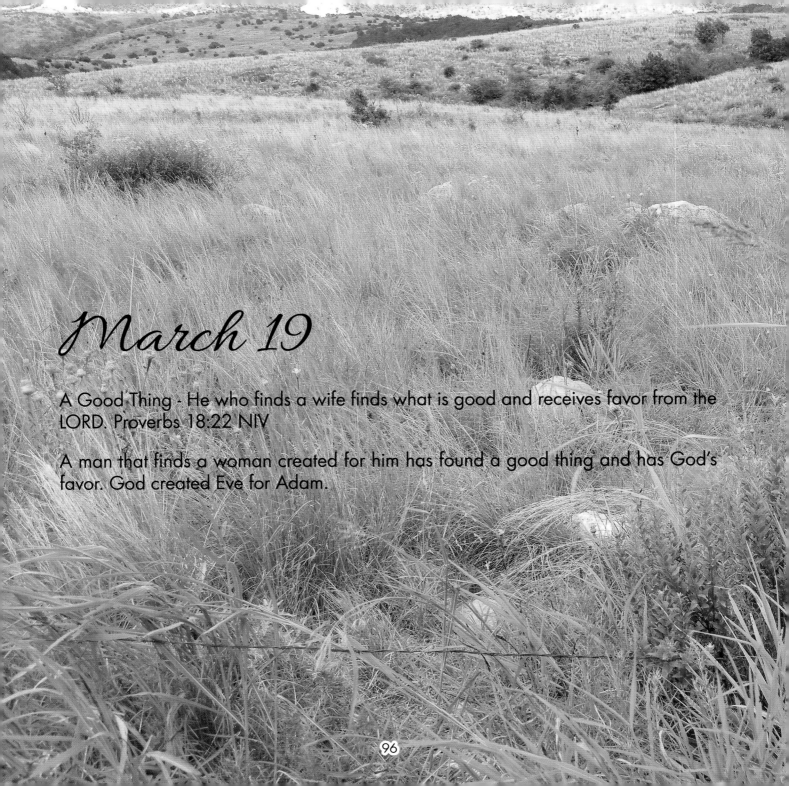

March 19

A Good Thing - He who finds a wife finds what is good and receives favor from the LORD. Proverbs 18:22 NIV

A man that finds a woman created for him has found a good thing and has God's favor. God created Eve for Adam.

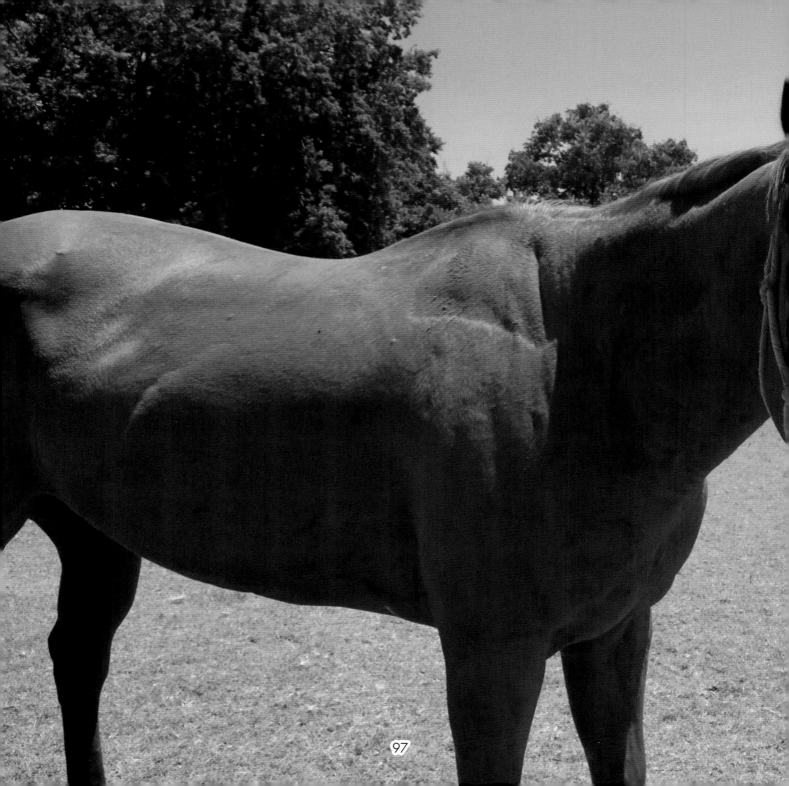

March 20

Generation To Generation - One generation shall praise Your works to another, And shall declare Your mighty acts. Psalm 145:4 NKJV

Praise and speak of His goodness to another generation.

March 21

God's Chosen People - Therefore, as God's chosen people, holy and dearly loved, clothe yourselves with compassion, kindness, humility, gentleness and patience. Colossians 3:12 NIV

As a chosen child of God, I will carry myself with love and compassion for all mankind.

March 22

Blessed - Blessed are they which do hunger and thirst after righteousness: for they shall be filled. Matthew 5:6 KJV

To earnestly seek after fulfillment to replenish your soul is a satisfying feeling.

March 23

Walk - Though I walk in the midst of trouble, You will revive me; You will stretch out Your hand Against the wrath of my enemies, and Your right hand will save me. Psalm 138:7 NKJV

You are the Preserver of my life. I have walked with trouble all around me and my enemies have come against me. You stretched out Your hand and saved me.

March 24

Anxiety - Cast all your anxiety on him because he cares for you. 1 Peter 5:7 NIV

If I give all my anxieties to the Lord, I should not have anxiety. That is easier said than done. But I must humble myself and know that God is bigger than any situation(s) in life that may come my way.

March 25

Blessed - Blessed in the one who does not walk in step with the wicked or stand in the way that sinner take or sit in the company of mockers, but whose delight is in the law of the LORD, and who meditates on his law day and night. Psalm 1:1-2 NIV

Watch what you are doing when you are walking, standing or sitting. I am blessed when I seek Godly counsel, when I avoid hanging out with sinners, and do not join in with mocking others. Keep meditating on God's Word.

March 26

Peace - Consider the blameless, observe the upright; a future awaits those who seek peace. Psalm 37:37 NIV

A man who serves and obeys God will have peace on this earth and forevermore.

March 27

Blessed - Blessed are those who mourn, For they shall
be comforted. Matthew 5:4 NKJV

You will be comforted whether you are mourning the
loss of a loved one, a current situation or mourning
over sin in your life.

March 28

Bless Them - Bless them which persecute you: bless, and curse not. Romans 12:14 KJV

We must continue to bless and pray for those you mean us harm.

March 29

Choose - This day I call the heavens and the earth as witnesses against you that I have set before you life and death, blessings and curses. Now choose life, so that you and your children may live and that you may love the LORD your God, listen to his voice, and hold fast to him. For the LORD is your life, and he will give you many years in the land he swore to give to your fathers, Abraham, Isaac, and Jacob. Deuteronomy 30:19-20 NIV

TODAY I CHOOSE LIFE!!

March 30

Walk - Whoever walks in integrity walks securely, but whoever takes crooked paths will be found out. Proverbs 10:9 NIV

Help me to walk in honesty so that my walk may be secure. If my walk is dishonest, please reveal it to me.

March 31

Plank In My Eye - How can you say to your brother, 'Let me take the speck out of your eye,' when all the time there is a plank in your own eye? Matthew 7:4 NIV

Do not be blind to your own sins before attempting to address the sins of your brother. You may not be walking the right path.

April 1

I will hear - I will hear what God the LORD will speak: for he will speak unto his people. And to his saints but let them not turn again to folly. Psalm 85:8 KJV

I recognize the guidance of the Holy Spirit by being familiar with God's Word. When God has released me from a stronghold, it is foolish for me to return back to the same stronghold.

April 2

Lifter - But you, LORD, are a shield around me, my glory, the One who lifts my head high. Psalm 3:3 NIV

When I remember the glory of the LORD and that the LORD is my shelter, my bowed

April 3

Perfect Peace - You will keep him in perfect peace, Whose mind is stayed on You, Because he trusts in You. Isaiah 26:3 NKJV

"Perfect Peace", a peace that surpasses all understanding. I have a promise from God that I can have perfect peace and be kept in perfect peace when my mind is on Him.

April 4

Peace - LORD, You will establish peace for us, For You have also done all our works in us. Isaiah 26:12 NKJV

You have given me peace and You have fulfilled all the works within me.

April 5

Plank In My Eye - "Why do you look at the speck of sawdust in your brother's eye and pay no attention to the plank in your own eye? Matthew 7:3 NIV

Before focusing on the fault of others, first, we need to address our own faults, which may be greater.

April 6

Walk - He who walks with wise men will be wise,
But the companion of fools will be destroyed.
Proverbs 13:20 NKJV

If I walk with wisdom, I will become wise. If I
partner with foolishness it will lead to my
destruction.

April 7

Hiding Place - You are my hiding place and my shield; I hope in Your word.
Psalm 119:114 NKJV

I get away from unhealthy thoughts in my mind by thinking of Jesus, my hiding place and shield. My hope is in Jesus.

April 8

Seek wisdom - I love them that love me; and those that seek me early shall find me. Proverbs 8:17 KJV

Seek wisdom. For wisdom is better than rubies; and all the things that may be desired are not to be compared to it. Proverbs 8:11 KJV. You must read Proverbs 8:1-36.

April 9

My Help – I will lift up my eyes to the hills – From whence comes my help? My help comes from the LORD, Who made heaven and earth. He will not allow your foot to be moved; He who keeps you will not slumber. Psalm 121:1-3 NKJV

He is my ever-present help!! He will watch over me both day and night.

April 10

Praise The Lord - From the rising of the sun to its going down The LORD's name is to be praised. Psalm 113:3 NKJV

Let everything that has breath praise the LORD. Praise the LORD! Psalm 150:6 NKJV. Did you wake up with praise on your lips? Will you go to bed with praise on your mind?

April 11

Be Still - Be still before the LORD and wait patiently for him; do not fret when people succeed in their ways, when they carry out their wicked schemes. Psalm 37:7 NIV

I will wait patiently, seeking and knowing that what God has for me is for me. I will receive in His time and not be concerned about the possessions of others and how they obtained it.

April 12

Peace - "The LORD bless you and keep you; The LORD make His face shine upon you, And be gracious to you; The LORD lift up His countenance upon you, And give you peace."' Numbers 6:24-26 NKJV

When I think of all the blessings I have received, seen and unseen I have peace. I will rest in the peace of the LORD.

April 13

Walk - Those who trust in themselves are fools, but those who walk in wisdom are kept safe.
Proverbs 28:26 NIV

Lord, when I am in need let me seek You and walk with You and not seek a path that is unjust.

April 14

Truth - For my mouth shall speak truth; and wickedness is an abomination to my lips. Proverbs 8:7 KJV

If I have accepted Him, I have accepted the truth. Jesus answered, "I am the way and the truth and the life. John 14:6a NIV. To speak evil to and about someone is doing the opposite of who He is. Seek wisdom and speak the truth or speak nothing at all.

April 15

Believe - Then Jesus told him, "Because you have seen me, you have believed; blessed are those who have not seen and yet have believed." John 20:29 NIV

We must live this Christian life with the faith that Jesus Christ is who He says He is. Our faith in Christ must not waver.

April 16

Be Strong - Be on your guard; stand firm in the faith; be courageous; be strong. 1 Corinthians 16:13 NIV

Be ready, stand firm in who your faith is in. Through His strength, you will be strong and have the courage to stand.

April 17

The Comforter - But the Comforter, which is the Holy Ghost, whom the Father will send in my name, he shall teach you all things, and bring all things to your remembrance, whatsoever I have said unto you. John 14:26 KJV

As I read and study Your Word, all things will be taught to me and brought to my

April 18

Blessing - The blessing of the LORD makes one rich, And He adds no sorrow with it. Proverbs 10:22 NKJV

A man's destiny to be rich by the will of God comes with no fear, greed, or worries.

April 19

Laughter And Joy - He will yet fill your mouth with laughter and your lips with shouts of joy.
Job 8:21 NIV

Bad things happen to people we know and love. But God can turn our mourning into laughter.

April 20

Walk - O house of Jacob, come and let us walk In the light of the LORD. Isaiah 2:5 NKJV

Take pleasure in walking in the light of the Lord and not walking with customs and traditions.

April 21

Abundantly Above - Now unto him that is able to do exceeding abundantly above all that we ask or think, according to the power that worketh in us, Ephesians 3:20 KJV

Just imagine your biggest dream, God can do abundantly above your thoughts through the Holy Spirit that is within you.

April 22

Rest - And He said, "My Presence will
go with you, and I will give you rest."
Exodus 33:14 NKJV

God is with us, rest in His presence.

April 23

Bond Of Peace - Make every effort to keep the unity of the Spirit through the bond of peace. Ephesians 4:3 NIV

I will do all I can to keep the Holy Spirit united, by being humble, longsuffering and patient. Help me to cease from acts and thoughts of revenge and connect me with others through peace.

April 24

Covenant Of Peace - For the mountains shall depart, and the hills be removed; but my kindness shall not depart from thee, neither shall the covenant of my peace be removed, saith the LORD that hath mercy on thee. Isaiah 54:10 KJV

Great are the mountains and hills, but in time they will erode, be removed or wither away. But I have an everlasting kindness and a covenant of peace with God.

April 25

The Gift Of God - For by grace are ye saved through faith; and that not of yourselves: it is the gift of God: Not of works, lest any man should boast. Ephesians 2:8-9 KJV

Salvation is a gift from God. We only have to have faith in God and accept the gift.

April 26

Delivered Me - I sought the LORD, and he heard me, and delivered me from all my fears. Psalm 34:4 KJV

When I seek the LORD earnestly, diligently and with my whole heart, He will hear my cry and answer me. The LORD will save me out of the hands of all my enemies, so I have no reason to fear.

April 27

Walk - Whether you turn to the right or to the left, your ears will hear a voice behind you, saying, "This is the way; walk in it." Isaiah 30:21 NIV

Help me to walk where Your Word directs me.

April 28

Serve - Serve wholeheartedly, as if you were serving the Lord, not people. Ephesians 6:7 NIV

Do your service with sincerity and faithfulness as unto the Lord, not for people.

April 29

We Shall Reap - And let us not be weary in well doing: for in due season we shall reap, if we faint not. Galatians 6:9 KJV

Don't get overwhelmed in your Christian walk. It takes time to reap from your labor. Pray for endurance.

April 30

Peace - My son, do not forget my teaching, but keep my commands in your heart, for they will prolong your life many years and bring you peace and prosperity. Proverbs 3:1-2 NIV

Keep the Word in your heart. The Word comes to my remembrance when I need it most. And It gives me peace. Living the Word will add days to my life.

To God be the Glory!!

May 1

Secret Place - But you, when you pray, go into your room, and when you have shut your door, pray to your Father who is in the secret place; and your Father who sees in secret will reward you openly. Matthew 6:6 NKJV

Go to your secret place and pray to the unseen God with omnipotent power to do anything but fail.

May 2

Victory Through Jesus Christ - But thanks be to God, who gives us the victory through our Lord Jesus Christ. 1 Corinthians 15:57 NKJV

I give thanks to God for sending His Son to die for our sins and rising on that third day morn with ALL power in his hand. We now have victory over sin and death, through Jesus Christ.

May 3

Understanding - The entrance of Your words gives light; It gives understanding to the simple. Psalm 119:130 NKJV

As Your Word enters into my heart, mind, and soul I am illuminated.

May 4

Renewed Strength - But they that wait upon the LORD shall renew their strength; they shall mount up with wings as eagles; they shall run, and not be weary; and they shall walk, and not faint. Isaiah 40:31 KJV

Am I renewing or gaining new strength? Am I rising above my problems in my walk for the LORD? My strength is from the LORD. As I wait on the LORD I will renew and gain new strength.

May 5

If My People - If my people, which are called by my name, shall humble themselves, and pray, and seek my face, and turn from their wicked ways; then will I hear from heaven, and will forgive their sin, and will heal their land. 2 Chronicles 7:14 KJV

God is waiting for us!!

May 6

Blessed - Blessed is the one whose transgressions are forgiven, whose sins are covered.
Psalm 32:1 NIV

I have accepted Jesus as my Lord and Savior and my sins are covered by His blood.

May 7

Deeds - But someone will say, "You have faith; I have deeds." Show me your faith without deeds, and I will show you my faith by my deeds. James 2:18 NIV

I cannot show evidence of my
faith without showing my works.
Faith without works is dead.

May 8

Peace - Let us therefore make every effort to do what leads to peace and to mutual edification. Romans 14:19 NIV

Make every effort to respond to all men in a loving and kind manner. Look for ways to encourage and strengthen one another.

May 9

Do Good - As we have therefore opportunity, let us do good unto all men, especially unto them who are of the household of faith. Galatians 6:10 KJV

At the appropriate time we must do good toward all mankind. Your appropriate time, may be now!!

May 10

Refuge - The LORD also will be a refuge for the oppressed, a refuge in times of trouble. Psalm 9:9 KJV

You will shelter me in my brokenness and in my times of tribulations.

May 11

Walk - He has shown you, O man, what is good; and what does the LORD require of you. But to do justly, To love mercy, and to walk humbly with your God? Micha 6:8 NKJV

I have been shown what is good and what the LORD requires of me, now it is up to me to walk in the right direction.

May 12

Mercy, Love And Peace - Mercy unto you, and peace, and love, be multiplied. Jude 1:2 KJV

Today I will show love, peace, and mercy to all mankind.

May 13

Favor - Let not mercy and truth forsake you; Bind them around your neck, Write them on the tablet of your heart, And so find favor and high esteem In the sight of God and man. Proverbs 3:3-4 NKJV

The virtues of mercy and truth that comes from God should be a part of my daily outward behavior toward everyone I encounter.

May 14

Distress - In my distress I cried unto the LORD, and he heard me. Psalm 120:1 KJV

In my moment of pain, I talked to the LORD and He responded to me.

May 15

A Time - a time to tear and a time to mend, a time to be silent and a time to speak,
Ecclesiastes 3:7 NIV

There is a time to respond or not to respond in every situation.

May 16

Peace - For ye shall go out with joy, and be led forth with peace: the mountains and the hills shall break forth before you into singing, and all the trees of the field shall clap their hands. Isaiah 55:12 KJV

Even the mountains and the hills and the trees will rejoice in my joy and peace.

May 17

No Other - That they may know from the rising of the sun, and from the west, that there is none beside me. I am the LORD, and there is none else. Isaiah 45:6 KJV

There is no other God, but You. Help me to proclaim Your goodness in all that I do.

May 18

Walk - Nevertheless I must walk to day, and to morrow, and the day following: for it cannot be that a prophet perish out of Jerusalem. Luke 13:33 KJV

I must continue to walk day after day in the way of the Lord until my time comes.

May 19

Praise - I will give You thanks in the great assembly; I will praise You among many people. Psalm 35:18 NKJV

I will tell of Your goodness to me in the congregation of saints. When an opportunity is presented, we should share our testimony.

May 20

Inspiration - One thing have I desired of the LORD, that will I seek after; that I may dwell in the house of the LORD all the days of my life, to behold the beauty of the LORD, and to enquire in his temple. Psalm 27:4 KJV

My soul shouts for joy when I imagine dwelling in the house of the LORD forevermore.

May 21

Continuous - I will bless the LORD at all times: his praise shall continually be in my mouth. Psalm 34:1 KJV

LORD, whatever state I am in, help me to praise Your holy name.

May 22

Depart From Evil - Do not be wise in your own eyes; fear the LORD and shun evil. This will bring health to your body and nourishment to your bones. Proverbs 3:7-8 NIV

We were created to be peaceful
and loving humans. Living life
with little or no stress will bring
healing to your body.

May 23

Hate - Hatred stirs up strife, But love covers all sins. Proverbs 10:12 NKJV

Hate is the opposite of what God is. Hate looks for ways to destroy and expose one's sin. Love looks for ways to lift others by covering their sin.

May 24

Peace With God - Therefore being justified by faith, we have peace with God through our Lord Jesus Christ. Romans 5:1 KJV

I am no longer a stranger to God because of my sins. I have been justified by faith and my relationship has been restored through our Lord Jesus Christ. I have peace with God.

May 25

Walk - Then Peter said, "Silver and gold I do not have, but what I do have I give you: In the name of Jesus Christ of Nazareth, rise up and walk." Acts 3:6 NKJV

I have nothing to give you, but Jesus Christ, learn of Him and walk.

May 26

Compassion - The LORD is good to all; he has compassion on all he has made. Psalm 145:9 NIV

The LORD's mercies endureth forevermore.

May 27

Peace Be Still - And he arose, and rebuked the wind, and said unto the sea, Peace, be still. And the wind ceased, and there was a great calm.
Mark 4:39 KJV

The Lord can speak peace to the winds and calm the roaring waves of the sea, and He can speak peace to my troubles and calm my soul.

May 28

Peace - And the God of peace shall bruise Satan under your feet shortly. The grace of our Lord Jesus Christ be with you. Amen. Romans 16:20 KJV

Satan will be destroyed and the God of Peace will reign!!

May 29

Nothing Too Hard For God - Behold, I am the LORD, the God of all flesh: is there any thing too hard for me? Jeremiah 32:27 KJV

Name one thing too hard for God.

May 30

Absent From The Body - We are confident, I say, and willing rather to be absent from the body, and to be present with the Lord. 2 Corinthians 5:8 KJV

It is a comfort knowing when loved ones have confessed their hope in Jesus Christ leave this world, they are in His presence.

May 31

Rest In God - Yes, my soul, find rest in God; my hope comes from him. Truly he is my rock and my salvation; he is my fortress, I will not be shaken. My salvation and my honor depend on God; he is a mighty rock, my refuge. Psalm 62:5-7 NIV

My rest is in God because I trust that He knows what is best for me. As I continue to trust Him, He will strengthen my foundation and I will not be moved.

June 1

Walk - Jesus said to him, "Rise, take up your bed and walk." John 5:8 NKJV

I will not dwell in the pit. I will rise up and walk into my promises. When you feel you are in a pit, find your promise in the Word. I will not be a pit dweller.

June 2

Peace And Sleep - I will both lay me down in peace, and sleep: for thou, LORD, only makest me dwell in safety. Psalm 4:8 KJV

I will sleep in peace, knowing that I will walk in peace today. God will keep me safe.

June 3

My Comfort - May your unfailing love be my comfort, according to your promise to your servant. Psalm 119:76 NIV

I am comforted by God's faithfulness and His promises to me.

June 4

The Just And Unjust - that you may be sons of your Father in heaven; for He makes His sun rise on the evil and on the good, and sends rain on the just and on the unjust. Matthew 5:45 NKJV

God provides for the just and the unjust. But God demonstrates his own love for us in this: While we were still sinners, Christ died for us. Romans 5:8 NIV.

June 5

Shining Light - But the path of the just is as the shining light, that shineth more and more unto the perfect day. Proverbs 4:18 KJV

As our knowledge of God grows, the light gets brighter and brighter until the day we can see the true Light.

June 6

Prayer - Devote yourselves to prayer, being watchful and thankful. Colossians 4:2 NIV

Prayer is one of the most intimate ways to connect with God. Dedicate some time to communicate with God, being grateful and on your guard. How is your prayer life?

June 7

Joy - Deceit is in the hearts of those who plot evil, but those who promote peace have joy. Proverbs 12:20 NIV

If I take action on the evil thoughts in my mind, I am deceiving myself if I think the outcome is going to be good for me. Blessed are the peacemakers.

June 8

Walk - So we are always confident, knowing that while we are at home in the body we are absent from the Lord. For we walk by faith, not by sight. 2 Corinthians 5:6-7 NKJV

I will be mindful to walk in complete trust. Believing that You God are all-knowing and You go before me. I will not walk by what I see.

June 9

Peace - the LORD turn his face toward you and give you peace."' Numbers 6:26 NIV

The LORD took my pain and gave me peace. What an exchange!!

June 10

Strength - The LORD is my light and my salvation; whom shall I fear? the LORD is the strength of my life; of whom shall I be afraid? Psalm 27:1 KJV

With the LORD on my side, why should I be fearful and afraid?

June 11

Gospel Of Peace - and with your feet fitted with the readiness that comes from the gospel of peace. Ephesians 6:15 NIV

My feet will be prepared to take the gospel of peace to others.

June 12

Ask, Seek, Knock - Ask, and it shall be given you; seek, and ye shall find; knock, and it shall be opened unto you: For every one that asketh receiveth; and he that seeketh findeth; and to him that knocketh it shall be opened. Matthew 7:7-8 KJV

Your opportunity to serve the Lord is waiting for you.

June 13

Greatest Love - For God so loved the world, that he gave his only begotten Son, that whosoever believeth in him should not perish, but have everlasting life. John 3:16 KJV

Because of God's love for the world, He gave up His only offspring so that believers in Him wouldn't perish, but have eternal life. The greatest love ever shown to me.

June 14

Peace - For God is not the author of confusion, but of peace, as in all churches of the saints.
1 Corinthians 14:33 KJV

213

Confusion is not created by God, but God can bring order to confusion.

June 15

Walk - For we are His workmanship, created in Christ Jesus for good works, which God prepared beforehand that we should walk in them. Ephesians 2:10 NKJV

As a new creature in Christ, I was created for good works. God has crafted me with the skills and with a purpose to do good works. Lord give me the strength to endure this walk.

June 16

Anger - A gentle answer turns away wrath, but a harsh word stirs up anger. Proverbs 15:1 NIV

Choose your words wisely and be soft in your delivery.

June 17

Wisdom - If any of you lacks wisdom, you should ask God, who gives generously to all without finding fault, and it will be given to you. James 1:5 NIV

If I abide in God's Word, I will have the ability to know the truth. In God's word is deep and secret things that only the believers have access to. Wisdom will prolong your life.

June 18

Support The Weak - I have shown you in every way, by laboring like this, that you must support the weak. And remember the words of the Lord Jesus, that He said, 'It is more blessed to give than to receive.'" Acts 20:35 NKJV

We are blessed to be a blessing to others. Help me to practice giving, as I have been shown. What can I give today to make someone's day better?

June 19

Helping Others - But whoever has this world's goods, and sees his brother in need, and shuts up his heart from him, how does the love of God abide in him? 1 John 3:17 NKJV

How can you say you love God and have the ability to help your bother and do not? Who has God put on your heart to help today?

June 20

Jehovah Shalom - So Gideon built an altar to the LORD there and called it The Lord Is Peace. To this day it stands in Ophah of the Abiezrites. Judges 6:24 NIV

I want the LORD of Peace to be present in my life so that generations to come will see His peace in me.

June 21

Word - In the beginning was the Word, and the
Word was with God, and the Word was God.
John 1:1 KJV

Jesus is the Word. In the beginning was Jesus, and Jesus was with God and Jesus was God.

June 22

Walk - I, therefore, the prisoner of the Lord, beseech you to walk worthy of the calling with which you were called, with all lowliness and gentleness, with longsuffering, bearing with one another in love, endeavoring to keep the unity of the Spirit in the bond of peace. Ephesians 4:1-3 NJKV

We must be found walking in our divine calling. We should be loving one another with lowliness, gentleness, and longsuffering.

June 23

Give me understanding - Your hands have made me and fashioned me; Give me understanding, that I may learn Your commandments. Psalm 119:73 NKJV

God, You are my creator. I seek Your help for an understanding of Your Word.

June 24

God's Daily drawings - The heavens declare the glory of God; the skies proclaim the work of his hands. Psalm 19:1 NIV

The sky reveals the glory of God, it shows His artwork. He continuously paints a different picture for our enjoyment both day and night. LOOK AT THE SKIES!!

June 25

Favor - Surely, LORD, you bless the righteous; you surround them with your favor as with a shield. Psalm 5:12 NIV

I have favor from the LORD because of His righteousness.

June 26

Light - When Jesus spoke again to the people, he said, "I am the light of the world. Whoever follows me will never walk in darkness, but will have the light of life." John 8:12 NIV

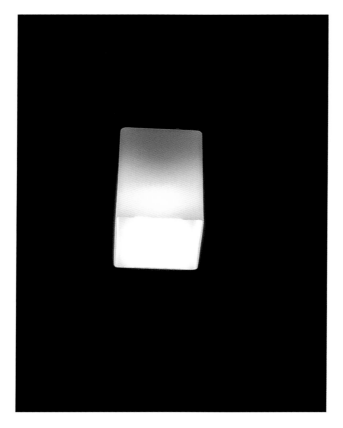

God's light will always be seen in darkness. Stop walking in darkness and let God light up your path.

June 27

Way Of Peace - To give light to them that set in darkness and in the shadow of death, to guide our feet into the way of peace. Luke 1:79 KJV

I am no longer a stranger to God because of my sins. I have been justified by faith and my relationship has been restored through our Lord Jesus Christ. I have peace with God.

June 28

Redemption - In whom we have redemption through his blood, the forgiveness of sins, according to the riches of his grace; Ephesians 1:7 KJV

We have been delivered through the blood of Christ. Christ was a sinless sacrifice for our sins and we have been forgiven.

June 29

Walk - See then that you walk circumspectly, not as fools but as wise, redeeming the time, because the days are evil. Therefore do not be unwise, but understand what the will of the Lord is. Ephesians 5:15-17 NKJV

To walk wisely, you must know what God's will is. God's will for us is to glorify Him with our walk in life. What we eat, drink and any deeds we do should be to the glory of God.

June 30

Vengeance - Dearly beloved, avenge not yourselves, but rather give place unto wrath: for it is written, Vengeance is mine; I will repay, saith the Lord. Romans 12:19 KJV

God will take care of the ones who wronged me. I am not going to feel good about hurting someone. The best revenge is just letting go and moving on.

July 1

Free- Therefore if the Son makes you free, you shall be free indeed. John 8:36 NKJV

The Son has set me free. I am undeniably free!!

July 2

Free - You, my brothers and sisters, were called to be free. But do not use your freedom to indulge the flesh; rather, serve one another humble in love. Galatians 5:13 NIV

You have been called to liberty, free from the bondage of rituals. But do not use your freedom to commit sin.

July 3

Freedom And Confidence - In him and through faith in him we may approach God with freedom and confidence. Ephesians 3:12 NIV

Because of my faith in Christ, I can approach the throne of grace with freedom and confidence.

July 4

Freedom - But whoever looks intently into the perfect law that gives freedom, and continues in it - not forgetting what they have heard, but doing it - they will be blessed in what they do. James 1:25 NIV

As I study God's instructions for living it gives me freedom. But I must remember what I have learned and be found doing it, then I will be blessed.

July 5

Trust - Let the morning bring me word of your unfailing love, for I have put my trust in you. Show me the way I should go, for to you I entrust my life.
Psalm 143:8 NIV

My life is in Your hand. I surrender all to You. I trust that You will keep me.

July 6

Walk - Brethren, join in following my example, and note those who so walk, as you have us for a pattern. Philippians 3:17 NKJV

Look at the example of other Godly people. Their walk should be imitating Christ.

July 7

You God - The day is yours, and yours also the night; you established the sun and moon. It was you who set all the boundaries of the earth; you made both summer and winter. Psalm 74:16-17 NIV

God has control over the day, night, sun, moon and the seasons. He can handle any circumstance in our lives.

July 8

Afraid - Whenever I am afraid, I will trust in You.
Psalm 56:3 NKJV

When fear enters my thoughts and eye gates, help me to think about You. I know You did not give me the spirit of fear. Help me to trust in You.

244

July 9

Do Good - Make sure that nobody pays back wrong for wrong, but always strive to do what is good for each other and for everyone else.
1 Thessalonians 5:15 NIV

Tit for tat is unproductive, toxic and will put a wedge between my relationship with God. I will spend my time seeking ways to do good unto all men.

July 10

Peace - But the fruit of the Spirit is love, joy, peace, forbearance, kindness, goodness, faithfulness, gentleness and self-control. Against such things there is no law. Galatians 5:22-23 NIV

These are the attributes of the Godly attitudes that characterize the daily living of only those who belong to God by faith through Jesus Christ. As a believer in Christ, I have each attribute, some characteristics or attitudes are shown more than others. I have received the fruit; I will take possession. What is my strength and what is my weakness?

July 11

Peace - When a man's ways please the LORD he maketh, even his enemies to be at peace with him. Proverbs 16:7 KJV

God can turn my enemies into friends.

July 12

Prosper - Beloved, I pray that you may prosper in all the things and be in health, just as your soul prospers. 3 John 1:2 NKJV

When you can truly say, "It is well with my soul", it will comfort you when you encounter health problems.

July 13

Walk - that you may walk worthy of the Lord, fully pleasing Him, being fruitful in every good work and increasing in the knowledge of God; Colossians 1:10 NKJV

We need to exercise our knowledge of God. As we exercise, we will want to increase our knowledge of God and walk worthy of Him.

July 14

Clean Heart - Create in me a clean heart, O God; and renew a right spirit within me. Psalm 51:10 KJV

Remove any stones from my heart and replace them with a heart of flesh. Return to me the right spirit within me.

July 15

New Heart - I will give you a new heart and put a new spirit within you; I will take the heart of stone out of your flesh and give you a heart of flesh. Ezekiel 36:26 NKJV

You have given me a new heart; the stony heart has been replaced with a heart of flesh. Your spirit is within me. Help me to love all mankind.

July 16

Be Strong - Be strong and take heart, all you who hope in the LORD. Psalm 31:24 NIV

My hope is in the LORD and through Him, my heart is strengthened and I am encouraged.

July 17

Mankind - what is mankind that you are mindful of them, human beings that you care for them? Psalm 8:4 NIV

Lord, I thank You for caring for me when I did not acknowledge it was You.

July 18

Hold Your Peace - The LORD shall fight for you, and ye shall hold your peace. Exodus 14:14 KJV

Help me to be obedient to the Lord by holding my peace and letting Him fight for me. He can handle it!!

258

July 19

My Mouth - Out of the same mouth come praise and cursing. My brothers and sisters, this should not be. James 3:10 NIV

We only have one mouth and out of it should flow blessings for all mankind. Lord help me to think before saying something harmful to another individual.

July 20

Walk - As you therefore have received Christ Jesus the Lord so walk in Him, rooted and built up in Him and established in the faith, as you have been taught, abounding in it with thanksgiving. Colossians 2:6-7 NKJV

It's all in your walk. Walk by your faith in the Lord showing thankfulness and gratitude.

July 21

My Ways - I have considered my ways and have turned my steps to your statutes. Psalm 119:59 NIV

As I look back over my life and considered my ways I turned to Your ways.

July 22

Beautify - For the LORD taketh pleasure in his people: he will beautify the meek with salvation. Psalm 149:4 KJV

Humble me LORD and let me know and do Your will.

July 23

My Strength - I can do all things through Christ who strengthens me. Philippians 4:13 NKJV

God tells us not to limit ourselves and do not be afraid. He will give us the strength and the ability to conquer whatever He calls us to do because it is His will.

July 24

Your Promise - My comfort in my suffering is this: Your promise preserves my life.
Psalm 119:50 NIV

Your blessed assurance gives me comfort in my suffering.

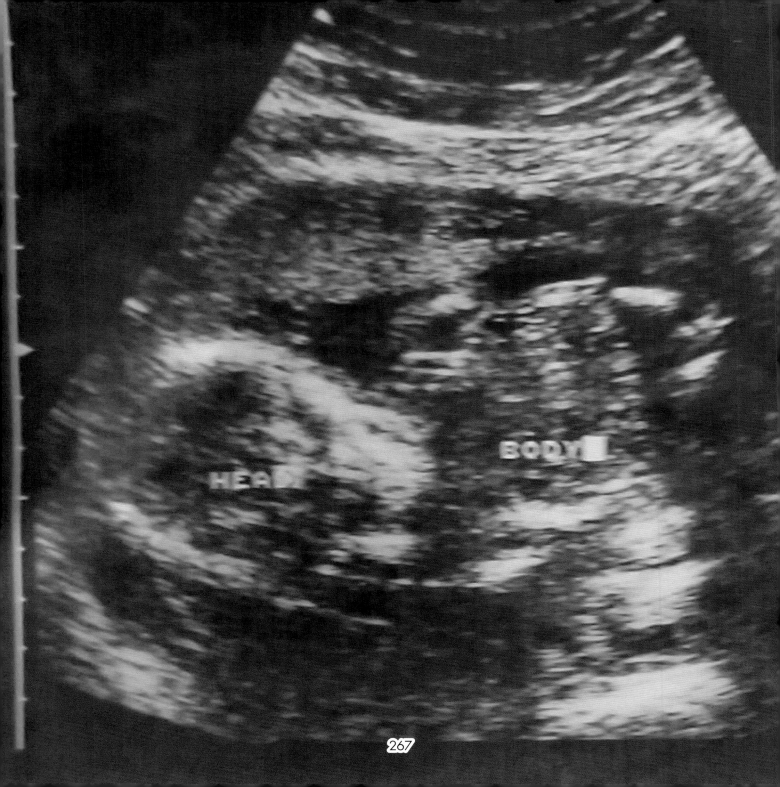

July 25

Wonderfully Made - I will praise You, for I am fearfully and wonderfully made; Marvelous are Your works, And that my soul knows very well. NKJV

I praise God, that I am unique and wonderfully made. His works are wonderful. I am created in His image with purpose and I have no doubt.

July 26

Love - This is My commandment, that you love one another as I have loved you. Greater love has no one than this, than to lay down one's life for his friends. John 15:12-13 NKJV

Unconditional love.

July 27

Walk - in which you yourselves once walked when you lived in them. But now you yourselves are to put off all these: anger, wrath, malice, blasphemy, filthy language out of your mouth. Colossians 3:7-8 NKJV

As a new creature in Christ, old things have passed away. Help me to restrain from anger, wrath, malice, blasphemy and filthy language from my mouth.

July 28

God Hears - I love the LORD, for he heard my voice; he heard my cry for mercy. Because he turned his ear to me, I will call on him as long as I live. Psalm 116:1-2 NIV

Because the Lord thought enough to turn his ear toward me, I will call on Him as long as I live.

July 29

My Soul - Yes, my soul, find rest in God; my hope comes from him. Psalm 62:5 NIV

My soul finds rest in God and my salvation comes from Him and Him alone.

273

July 30

Majestic Is Your Name - LORD, our Lord, how majestic is your name in all the earth! You have set your glory in the heavens. Through the praise of children and infants you have established a stronghold against your enemies, to silence the foe and the avenger. When I consider your heavens, the work of your fingers, the moon and the stars, which you have set in place, what is mankind that you are mindful of them, human beings that you care for them? You have made them a little lower than the angels and crowned them with glory and honor. You made them rulers over the works of your hands; you put everything under their feet: all flocks and herds, and the animals of the wild, the birds in the sky, and the fish in the sea, all that swim the paths of the seas. LORD, our Lord, how majestic is your name in all the earth! Psalm 8:1-9 NIV

July 31

Bless You Abundantly - And God is able to bless you abundantly, so that in all things at all times, having all that you need, you will abound in very good work.
2 Corinthians 9:8 NIV

Help me to see the abundant blessings of God in all things. As I do Your good work, show me Your sufficient supply of everything I need.

August 1

Laughter - A merry heart does good, like medicine, But a broken spirit dries the bones. Proverbs 17:22 NKJV

Laughter can be healing and preservation to the body, but a defeated spirit can drain the strength from the body.

August 2

Be Strong And Very Courageous - "Be strong and very courageous. Be careful to obey all the law my servant Moses gave you; do not turn from it to the right or to the left, that you may be successful wherever you go. Keep the Book of the Law always on your lip; meditate on it day and night, so that you may be careful to do everything written in it. Then you will be prosperous and successful. Have I not commanded you? Be strong and courageous. Do not be afraid; do not be discouraged, for the LORD your God will be with you wherever you go." Joshua 1:7-9 NIV

August 3

Walk - that you would walk worthy of God who calls you into His own kingdom and glory. 1 Thessalonians 2:12 NKJV

We should live in a way that honors God. We have been chosen for His kingdom and glory. Today I will walk in the way that God rightfully deserves from me.

August 4

Love Your Enemies - But love your enemies, do good to them, and lend to them without expecting to get anything back. Then your reward will be great; and you will be children of the Most High, because he is kind to the ungrateful and wicked. Be merciful, just as your Father is merciful. Luke 6:35-36 NIV

Show mercy even to your enemies. Show love even to your enemies. We must not confront evil with evil, in doing so, our reward will be great.

August 5

Mind Your Own Business - that you also aspire to lead a quiet life, to mind your own business, and to work with your own hands, as we commanded you,
1 Thessalonians 4:11 NKJV

I will not be a gossiper; I will seek after living a life of quietness and mind my own business and let my hands be used to edify.

August 6

Do Not Worry - But seek first his Kingdom and his righteousness, and all these things will be given to you as well. Therefore do not worry about tomorrow, for tomorrow will worry about itself. Each day has enough trouble of its own. Matthew 6:33-34 NIV

Spend your time in God's Word and in prayer. He will take care of your necessities.

August 7

Meditate - Cause me to understand the way of our precepts, that I may meditate on your wonderful deeds. Psalm 119:27 NIV

Help me to understand Your order that I may think and speak on Your amazing works.

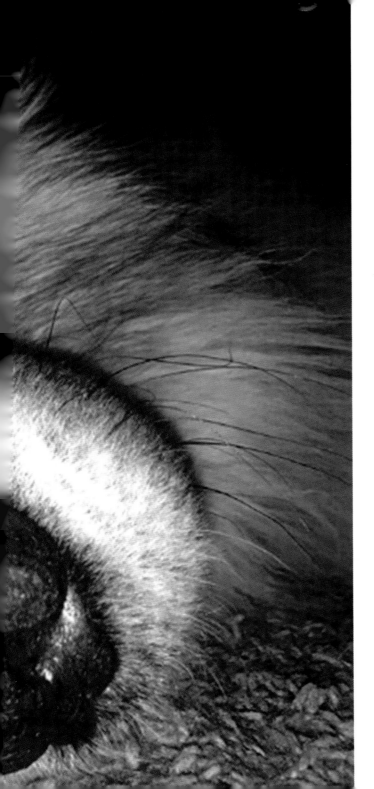

August 8

Peace - And the fruit of righteousness is sown in peace of them that make peace. James 3:18 KJV

I will reap what I sow. As I sow the seed of peace, I will reap the fruit of righteousness.

August 9

All Our Days - O satisfy us early with thy mercy; that we may rejoice and be glad all our days. Psalm 90:14 KJV

God's mercies are renewed every morning and will meet our needs.

August 10

Walk - Finally then, brethren, we urge and exhort in the Lord Jesus that you should abound more and more, just as you received from us how you ought to walk and to please God; 1 Thessalonians 4:1 NKJV

This is a lifelong walk. As we get closer and closer to God, we will learn the steps to take and the direction to go.

August 11

Reflection - Examine yourselves to see whether you are in the faith; test yourselves. Do you not realize that Christ Jesus is in you - unless, of course, you fail the test? 2 Corinthians 13:5 NIV

Are you a reflection of Jesus Christ? Jesus, I want to look more and more like You.

August 12

Trouble - We are troubled on every side, yet not distressed; we are perplexed, but not in despair; Persecuted, but not forsaken; cast down, but not destroyed; 2 Corinthians 4:8-9 KJV

Trouble is all around us, when life knocks us down, we have the strength to get back up. We can continue the fight because we will not be destroyed.

August 13

No Condemnation - Therefore, there is now no condemnation for those who are in Christ Jesus, because through Christ Jesus the law of the Spirit who gives life has set you free from the law of sin and death. Romans 8:1-2 NIV

Jesus Christ has set me free and I am not judged by the law. I will not give in to what my flesh wants, but walk in the spirit and live in the freedom that God has given me from the law of sin and death.

August 14

Seek Peace - Do not repay evil with evil or insult with insult. On the contrary, repay evil with blessing, because to this you were called so that you may inherit a blessing. For, "Whoever would love life and see good days must keep their tongue from evil and their lips from deceitful speech. They must turn from evil and do good; they must seek peace and pursue it. 1 Peter 3:9-11 NIV

Even when treated with evilness my desire should be to give a blessing in return. I will be rewarded for my actions. When I am in a bad situation, I will look for peace. God's peace within me will not be disturbed.

August 15

Happy - He who heeds the word wisely will find good, And whoever trusts in the LORD, happy is he. Proverbs 16:20 NKJV

O taste and see that the LORD is good: blessed is the man that trusteth in him. Psalm 34:8 KJV

August 16

Peacemakers - Blessed are the peacemakers: for they shall be called the children of God. Matthew 5:9 KJV

As a child of God, I should show myself as a peacemaker. I should be found actively bringing the conflict to an end as I carry the message of peace to others.

August 17

Walk - that you may walk properly toward those who are outside, and that you may lack nothing. 1 Thessalonians 4:12 NKJV

We must show Non-Christians how to walk the Christian walk.

August 18

Wait - Lead me in Your truth and teach me, For You are the God of my salvation; On You I wait all the day. Psalm 25:5 NKJV

From sun up to sundown, every day I wait on You to help me to be led by Your truth and teachings.

August 19

Peace - For I know the thoughts that I think toward you, saith the LORD, thoughts of peace, and not of evil, to give you an expected end. Jeremiah 29:11 KJV

God has a plan for my life, and even though I get off the path, He never throws my plan away. I now realize when I follow His plan, I prosper.

August 20

Encourage - Therefore encourage one another and build each other up, just as in fact you are doing. 1 Thessalonians 5:11 NIV

Today, I will speak words of encouragement.

August 21

Do What Is Needed - if it is to encourage, then give encouragement; if it is giving, then give generously; if it is to lead, do it diligently; if it is to show mercy, do it cheerfully. Romans 12:8 NIV

Once we have excepted Jesus Christ as our Lord and Savior, we receive spiritual gifts through God's Spirit. If you have these gifts you are to use them to serve.

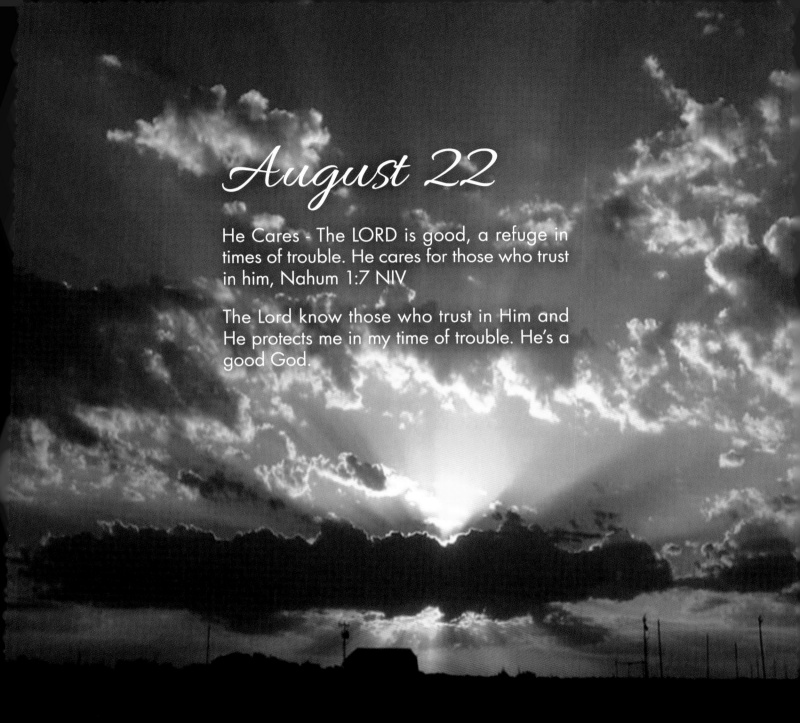

August 22

He Cares - The LORD is good, a refuge in times of trouble. He cares for those who trust in him, Nahum 1:7 NIV

The Lord know those who trust in Him and He protects me in my time of trouble. He's a good God.

August 23

Showers Of Blessings - I will make them and the places surrounding my hill a blessing. I will send down showers in season; there will be showers of blessing. Ezekiel 34:26 NIV

Rain down on me Your shower of blessings.

August 24

Walk - But we command you, brethren, in the name of our Lord Jesus Christ, that you withdraw from every brother who walks disorderly and not according to the tradition which he received from us. 2 Thessalonians 3:6 NKJV

Our walk should not be disorderly. God is not the author of confusion and we should not be a part of it. Just walk away!!

August 25

Old Age - They shall still bear fruit in old age; They shall be fresh and flourishing, To declare that the LORD is upright; He is my rock, and there is no unrighteousness in Him. Psalm 92:14-15 NKJV

I will remain in Him and in my old age continue to bear fruit and speak of the goodness of the LORD.

August 26

New Creature - Therefore if any man be in Christ, he is a new creature: old things are passed away; behold, all things are become new. 2 Corinthians 5:17 KJV

I am a new creature because I am in Christ. The things I use to do I do not do anymore. Witness the newness in me.

August 27

I Live - I am crucified with Christ: nevertheless I live; yet not I, but Christ liveth in me: and the life which I now live in the flesh I live by the faith of the Son of God, who loved me, and gave himself for me. Galatians 2:20 KJV

God gave Himself for me, because of His death, burial, and resurrection He lives in me. Therefore, I live by faith.

August 28

Jehovah - That men may know that thou, whose name alone is JEHOVAH, art the most high over all the earth.
Psalm 83:18 KJV

I know in Your time You will show just who You are!!

August 29

My Prayer - My voice shalt thou hear in the morning, O LORD; in the morning will I direct my prayer unto thee, and will look up. Psalm 5:3 KJV

When I start a new day, I will look up and pray unto You and You will hear my voice.

August 30

Teach Me - I will instruct you and teach you in the way you should go; I will guide you with My eye. Psalm 32:8 NKJV

You know what plans You have for me. Help me to see You as You lead the way.

August 31

Walk - Be sober, be vigilant, because your adversary the devil walks about like a roaring lion, seeking whom he may devour. 1 Peter 5:8 NKJV

The enemy walks around seeking to tear me down. I will keep my mind clear and watchful and be firm in my faith so I will not be destroyed by his tactics.

To God be the Glory!!

September 1

Fight - The LORD shall fight for you, and ye shall hold your peace. Exodus 14:14 KJV

The battle is not mine it is the LORD's. I will get behind the Lord and let him fight my battle.

September 2

Do Not Fear - So do not fear, for I am with you; do not be dismayed, for I am your God. I will strengthen you and help you; I will uphold you with my righteous right hand. Isaiah 41:10 NIV

In this life I may go through the fire and the water, I may even pass through the valley of the shadow of death, but I know my God is with me through it all.

September 3

Help When Needed - God is not unjust; he will not forget your work and the love you have shown him as you have helped his people and continue to help them. Hebrews 6:10 NIV

When we help others, we show love toward God and man. Has someone been put on your heart to help?

September 4

Love Your Enemies - But I say unto you which hear, Love your enemies, do good to them which hate you, Bless them that curse you, and pray for them which despitefully use you. Luke 6:27-28 KJV

This is a hard task, but through prayer it is attainable. Start praying for an individual that has done you harm and watch God soften your heart toward them.

September 5

Help From God - For I am the LORD your God who takes hold of your right hand and says to you, Do not fear; I will help you. Isaiah 41:13 NIV

God did not give me a spirit of fear. He will always be there to hold my hand and help me.

September 6

Think - Finally, brethren, whatsoever things are true, whatsoever things are honest, whatsoever things are just, whatsoever things are pure, whatsoever things are lovely, whatsoever things are of good report; if there be any virtue, and if there be any praise, think on these things. Philippians 4:8 KJV

Find what is true, honorable, just, pure, lovely, of good report, worthy of praise and of virtue and think on those things. I will meditate on these things and renew my mind.

September 7

Walk - But if we walk in the light as He is in the light, we have fellowship with one another, and the blood of Jesus Christ His Son cleanses us from all sin. 1 John 1:7 NKJV

As a child of the light, walking in the light will show in my living as He is the light. As I fellowship with Him you will see continuous cleansing and the fruit of my fellowship with Him.

September 8

Sustain Me- Even to your old age and gray hairs I am he, I am he who will sustain you. I have made you and I will carry you; I will sustain you and I will rescue you. Isaiah 46:4 NIV

When I am old and my hair is gray, He will continue to sustain me.

September 9

Love - Do everything in love. 1 Corinthians 16:14 NIV

God is love, and I am His Ambassador. So, as I represent Him, love should follow everything I do.

September 10

Be Generous - You will be enriched in every way so that you can be generous on every occasion, and through us your generosity will result in thanksgiving to God. 2 Corinthians 9:11 NIV

God has blessed you to be a blessing to others. When we bless others the glory and thanksgiving go to God.

328

September 11

Press On - Brethren, I do not count myself to have apprehended; but one thing I do, forgetting those things which are behind and reaching forward to those things which are ahead, I press toward the goal for the prize of the upward call of God in Christ Jesus. Philippians 3:13-14 NKJV

Press on!! Look forward!! Continue to move forward in a determined way until you reach your goal.

330

September 12

Joy And Peace - May the God of hope fill you with all joy and peace as you trust in him, so that you may overflow with hope by the power of the Holy Spirit. Romans 15:13 NIV

As my trust increases in God, I receive the blessing of hope, joy, peace, and power from the God of hope, joy, peace and power.

September 13

Peace - Great peace have they which love thy law: and nothing shall offend them. Psalm 119:165 KJV

Not only can I have peace in my life, but I can have great peace. As I continue to read, meditate, and study His Word, and as I start to love His law, I will accept His promise of great peace and nothing will vex me.

September 14

Walk - He who says he abides in Him ought himself also to walk just as He walked.
1 John 2:6 NKJV

If I say I accept Him, I must strive to walk like Him.

September 15

Supply All Your Needs - But my God shall supply all your needs according to his riches in glory by Christ Jesus. Philippians 4:19 KJV

God will supply ALL your needs whether it be tangible or intangible.

September 16

Faithful And Just - If we confess our sins, he is faithful and just to forgive us our sins, and to cleanse us from all unrighteousness. 1 John 1:9 KJV

I confessed, He remained faithful and just and forgave me of all my unrighteous ways. Thank You, Jesus!!

September 17

Power - He gives power to the weak, And to those who have no might He increases strength. Isaiah 40:29 NKJV

When I was weary and weak, You strengthen me. It is not by my might, but Your strength within me.

September 18

Healed - He said to her, "Daughter, your faith has healed you. Go in peace and be freed from your suffering." Mark 5:34 NIV

Jesus can heal you from your afflictions and save your soul.

September 19

A Prayer - By day the LORD directs his love, at night his song is with me - a prayer to the God of my life. Psalm 42:8 NIV

The LORD is 24/7 on-time God, waiting for us to reach out to Him through prayer.

September 20

Trust - Trust in the LORD with all thine heart; and lean not unto thine own understanding. In all thy ways acknowledge him and he shall direct thy paths. Proverbs 3:5-6 KJV

God's ways are above my ways and His thoughts are above my thoughts. My understanding is limited by my limitations. I will trust in God, He knows what is best for me.

September 21

Walk - It has given me great joy to find some of your children walking in the truth, just as the Father commanded us. 2 John 1:4 NIV

Does God find pleasure in my daily walk? What can I do to please Him today?

September 22

Return - Let us examine our ways and test them, and let us turn to the LORD.
Lamentations 3:40 NIV

How would you rate if your Christian walk was put to the test? Let's continue to seek the LORD by reading His Word.

September 23

Unwholesome Talk - Do not let any unwholesome talk come out of your mouths, but only what is helpful for building others up according to their needs, that it may benefit those who listen. Ephesians 4:29 NIV

Help me to represent you in my conversations, and remember everything You created was good.

September 24

In Prayer - Therefore I tell you, whatever you ask for in prayer, believe that you have received it, and it will be yours. Mark 11:24 NIV

Whatever you ask for that's in God's will for you will be granted unto you. If we do not know God's will, we know that He knows what I best for us.

September 25

You Are My Praise - Heal me, O LORD, and I shall be healed; Save me, and I shall be saved, For You are my praise. Jeremiah 17:14 NKJV

I will continue to praise You at all times for I know that You only can heal and save me.

September 26

Restores - The LORD sustains them on their sickbed and restores them from their bed of illness. Psalm 41:3 NIV

The LORD will comfort me in my bed of afflictions as He restores me back to my original condition.

September 27

Peace - Let the peace of Christ rule in your hearts, since as members of one body you were called to peace. And be thankful. Colossians 3:15 NIV

Believers are called to live in peace. An attribute of the fruit of the Spirit is peace. I have within my heart a desire to live in peace.

September 28

Walk - And this is love: that we walk in obedience to his commands. As you have heard from the beginning, his command is that you walk in love. 2 John 1:6 NIV

God is love; it is up to me to walk love out according to His Word.

September 29

Live Long - "Honor your father and your mother, so that you may live long in the land the LORD your God is giving you. Exodus 20:12 NIV

As I honor You, help me to follow your commands to honor others, that I may live long in the land You have given me.

September 30

Knowledge Of Him - Grace and peace be yours
in abundance through the knowledge of God and
of Jesus our Lord. His divine power has given us
everything we need for a godly life through our
knowledge of him who called us by his own glory
and goodness. 2 Peter 1:2-3 NIV

Through an intimate relationship with God, and
Jesus our Lord, we have what we need to never fall.

October 1

Grace, Love And Communion - The grace of the Lord Jesus Christ, and the love of God, and the communion of the Holy Ghost, be with you all, Amen. 2 Corinthians 13:14 KJV

Remember that God, the Lord Jesus Christ, and the Holy Spirit is with you.

October 2

In The Morning - And in the morning, rising up a great while before day, he went out, and departed into a solitary place, and there prayed. Mark 1:35 KJV

In the morning when I rise up, I want to spend time with You.

October 3

Let Your Light Shine - Let your light so shine before men, that they may see your good works, and glorify your Father which is in heaven. Matthew 5:16 KJV

What a great feeling when you know that others are glorying God Almighty because we let the light of Jesus shine in us.

October 4

Peace - Do not be anxious about anything, but in every situation, by prayer and petition, with thanksgiving, present your requests to God. And the peace of God, which transcends all understanding, will guard your hearts and your minds in Christ Jesus. Philippians 4:6-7 NIV

Addressing the problems in our lives should begin with prayer. The more you trust in God the less anxiety you will have. A peace that surpasses all understanding has to be experienced, it cannot be fully explained.

October 5

Walk - For I rejoiced greatly when brethren came and testified of the truth that is in you, just as you walk in the truth. 3 John 1:3 NKJV

Do you encourage others occasionally and speak on how they walk in truth? Will someone testify of your faithfulness in the truth?

October 6

You Lord - But you, Lord, are a compassionate and gracious God, slow to anger, abounding in love and faithfulness. Psalm 86:15 NIV

O Lord, You have shown me Your abundance in mercy and truth.

October 7

Good Courage - Be of good courage, and he shall strengthen your heart; all ye that hope in the LORD. Psalm 31:24 KJV

My hope is in the LORD and through Him, my heart is strengthened and I am encouraged.

October 8

My God - The God of my strength, in whom I will trust; My shield and the horn of my salvation, My stronghold and my refuge; My Savior, You save me from violence. I will call upon the LORD, who is worthy to be praised; So shall I be saved from my enemies. 2 Samuel 22:3-4 NKJV

The God of my strength is trustworthy; therefore, I will continue to call upon Him. He is worthy to be praised!!

October 9

Heart's Desire - May He grant you according to your heart's desire, And fulfill all your purpose. Psalm 20:4 NKJV

God will grant you the desires of your heart and you can fulfill your purpose according to His will.

October 10

Above All - For the LORD is a great God, and a great King above all gods. Psalm 95:3 KJV

For He is LORD of Lords, King of kings and God of gods!!

October 11

Blessed - O taste and see that the LORD is good: blessed is the man that trusteth in him. Psalm 34:8 KJV

If you do not ever try Him, you will never know how good He is. Try God, and trust in Him.

October 12

Walk - I have no greater joy than to hear that my children walk in truth, 3 John 1:4 NKJV

It is a blessing when someone you know is walking out their faith in the truth.

October 13

Peace - These things I have spoken unto you, that in me ye might have peace. In the world ye shall have tribulation: but be of good cheer; I have overcome the world. John 16:33 KJV

He has already overcome the world; I'm just celebrating in the victory.

October 14

A Light To My Path - Your word is a lamp to my feet And a light to my path.
Psalm 119:105 NKJV

When situations around me start getting dem or dark, Your Word brightens my path and I can see my way through.

October 15

Give Thanks - In every thing give thanks: for this is the will of God in Christ Jesus concerning you. 1 Thessalonians 5:18 KJV

I cannot always give thanks for everything but I can always give thanks in everything. I will trust that God knows what is best for me. Whatever comes in my life comes in by the will of God, otherwise, He would keep it from occurring.

October 16

God Of Peace - Those things, which ye have both learned, and received, and heard, and seen in me, do: and the God of peace shall be with you. Philippians 4:9 KJV

The bible is my guide for Christian living. I will not be just a hearer of the Word, but I must live the Word. In doing so, I will have the peace of God. Am I living by example?

October 17

Words Can Be Harmful - What goes into someone's mouth does not defile them, but what comes out of their mouth, that is what defile them." Matthew 15:11 NIV

Will the words that I speak show who I am or who I'm not?

October 18

Depart From Me - Depart from me, ye evildoers: for I will keep the commandments of my God. Psalm 119:115 KJV

Sometimes you have to remove yourself from the presence of offenders of God's law.

October 19

Walk - If we say that we have fellowship with Him, and walk in darkness, we lie and do not practice the truth. 1 John 1:6 NKJV

If I have fellowship with God, I should not have to tell you, you will see it in my walk. If I walk in darkness and tell you I fellowship with God, you will see that there is no truth in my walk.

October 20

He will Respond - I call out to the LORD, and he answers me from his holy mountain.
Psalm 3:4 NIV

When we give utterance unto the LORD, He will respond.

October 21

Cry Out - Then they cry unto the LORD in their trouble, and he bringeth them out to their distresses. Psalm 107:28 KJV

I have cried out to the Lord when I was troubled and He bought me out of my sorrow.

October 22

Praise You - For what you have done I will always praise you in the presence of your faithful people. And I will hope in your name, for your name is good. Psalm 52:9 NIV

I will praise You now and forevermore. You will make my enemies leave me alone. I will speak of Your goodness and praise Your holy name before Your people.

382

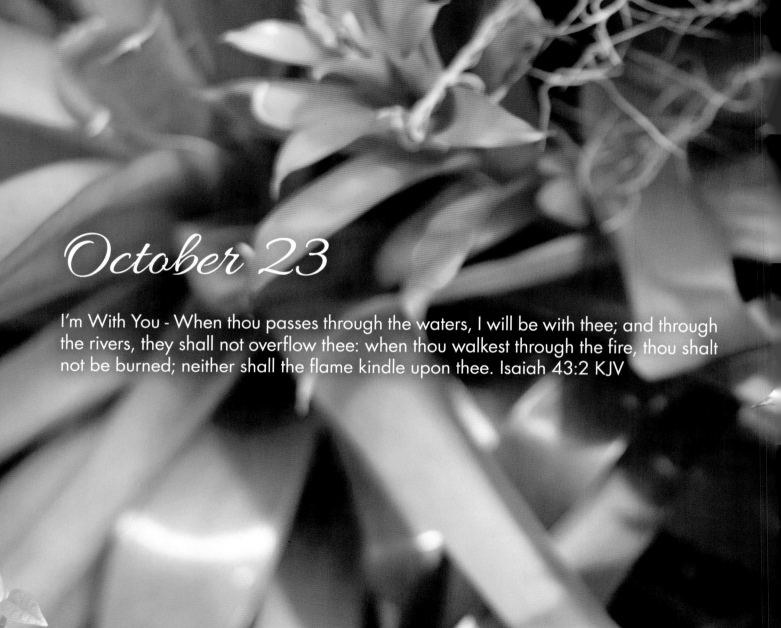

October 23

I'm With You - When thou passes through the waters, I will be with thee; and through the rivers, they shall not overflow thee: when thou walkest through the fire, thou shalt not be burned; neither shall the flame kindle upon thee. Isaiah 43:2 KJV

Nothing catches God by surprise. He goes before me. Nothing will overtake me. Because He is with me.

October 24

All Men - If it be possible, as much as lieth in you, live peaceably with all men. Romans 12:18 KJV

It is not always possible to live peaceable with all men, but it should be my desire to try to do all that is within me to live a peaceful life.

October 25

The Way - Jesus answered, "I am the way and the truth and the life. No one comes to the Father except through me. John 14:6 NIV

Jesus Christ is the Mediator between God and man. You must accept and believe that Jesus Christ is who He says He is. The only way to God.

October 26

Walk - And walk in love, as Christ also has loved us and given Himself for us, an offering and a sacrifice to God for a sweet-smelling aroma. Ephesians 5:2 NKJV

Help me to walk in love, honoring and giving myself to others, so that You will be glorified by the way I walk.

October 27

Silence -My dear brothers and sisters, take note of this: Everyone should be quick to listen, slow to speak and slow to become angry, James 1:19 NIV

If I listen to understand the speaker and not to respond I will be slower to speak.

October 28

The Tongue - The tongue of the wise adorns knowledge, but the mouth of the fool gushes folly. Proverbs 15:2 NIV

A wise man speaks at the appropriate time, but a foolish man speaks foolishness continually.

October 29

Peace - The LORD will give strength unto his people; the LORD will bless his people with peace. Psalm 29:11 KJV

My strength is through my Lord Christ Jesus. Peace is a promise from God. He will do great things.

October 30

Learn - It was good for me to be afflicted so that
I might learn your decrees. Psalm 119:71 NIV

In my moment of pain, Your Word draws me closer
to You and I am blessed.

October 31

Spirit Of Fear - For God has not given us the spirit of fear; but of power, and of love, and of a sound mind. 2 Timothy 1:7 KJV

I have within me the Holy Spirit; therefore, I have power, love, and self-discipline.

November 1

Live Peaceably - Recompense to no man evil for evil. Provide things in the sight of all men. If it be possible, as much as lieth in you, live peaceable with all men. Romans 12:17-18 KJV

I am not to repay evil done to me. I should live blameless in the sight of man. This comes about by knowing and living the Word of God.

November 2

Walk - This man heard Paul speaking. Paul, observing him intently and seeing that he had faith to be healed, said with a loud voice, "Stand up straight on your feet!" And he leaped and walked. Acts 14:9-10 NKJV

If I was being observed, would my faith show in my walk? Where am I in my faith walk? Do I walk by what I see or do I walk by faith?

November 3

Watch What You Say - Whoever guards his mouth and tongue Keeps his soul from troubles. Proverbs 21:23 NKJV

We can say and write things that can get us into trouble. You can damage your reputation and the reputation of others with our tongue. If your words are not edifying, they do not need to be spoken or written.

November 4

Peace - Peace I leave with you, my peace I give unto you: not as the world giveth, give I unto you. Let not your heart be troubled, neither let it be afraid. John 14:27 KJV

Peace is a gift from God. With God's peace within me, I have no room for fear.

November 5

To My Mother - Honor her for all that her hands have done, and let her works bring her praise at the city gate. Proverbs 31:31 NIV

I give honor to my mother. I asked my 93-year-old mom what was her favorite scripture she stated, "Psalm 23" and she quoted the first verse and she said, "And I believe every word of it." Is He your Shepherd?

November 6

Love - We love him, because he first loved us.
1 John 4:19 KJV

He died to show His love for me, knowing that I am not worthy but He sees value in me. His love has no limit. That gives me a reason to love Him even more.

November 7

The Works of God - As he went along, he saw a man blind from birth. His disciples asked him, "Rabbi, who sinned, this man or his parents, that he was born blind?" "Neither this man nor his parents sinned," said Jesus, "but this happened so that the works of God might be displayed in him. John 9:1-3 NIV

We have to play the hand we were dealt. Are you letting the works of God be revealed through you in your current circumstance?

November 8

Give Abundantly - Give, and it will be given to you. A good measure, pressed down, shaken together, and running over, will be poured into your lap. For with the measure you use, it will be measured to you." Luke 6:38 NIV

You should always be giving grace and forgiving others. The way you treat others is the way you will be treated.

405

November 9

Walk - Now in the fourth watch of the night Jesus went to them, walking on the sea. Matthew 14:25 NKJV

As you walk on the waves of life, Jesus will come to you and comfort you. You just have to doubt not, keep your eyes on Jesus and just keep walking!!

November 10

Restored - And the LORD restored Job's losses when he prayed for his friends. Indeed the LORD gave Job twice as much as he had before. Job 42:10 NKJV

The LORD can restore you to a better state mentally, spiritually, physically and financially.

November 11

Walk - For the LORD gives wisdom; From His mouth come knowledge and understanding; He stores up sound wisdom for the upright; He is a shield to those who walk uprightly; Proverbs 2:6-7 NKJV

Walking uprightly, I will receive some benefits only He could offer. He gives me wisdom. Some doors will be closed and some doors will be opened, just for me.

November 12

Book Of The Law - This Book of the Law shall not depart from your mouth, but you shall meditate in it day and night, that you may observe to do according to all that is written in it. For then you will make your way prosperous, and then you will have good success. Joshua 1:8 NKJV

God commanded Joshua to keep the Book of the Law on his lips and to meditate on His Word. We are charged to do the same and we will have good success.

November 13

Rejoicing - For his anger lasts only a moment, but his favor lasts a lifetime; weeping may stay for the night, but rejoicing comes in the morning. Psalm 30:5 NIV

Trouble don't last always!! There is sorrow in darkness but joy and rejoicing in the light. Favor from the LORD is forevermore.

November 14

Well Done - His lord said to him, 'Well done, good and faithful servant; you were faithful over a few things, I will make you ruler over many things. Enter into the joy of your lord.' Matthew 25:21 NKJV

When it is all over, I want to be on the right hand. I want the Lord to say, "Well done my good and faithful servant, enter into the gates of the Lord for you have been fervent."

November 15

Nothing Shall Separate Me - For I am persuaded, that neither death, nor life, nor angels, nor principalities, nor powers, nor things present, nor things to come, Nor height, nor depth, nor any other creature, shall be able to separate us from the love of God, which is in Christ Jesus our Lord. Romans 8:38-39 KJV

There is NOTHING that can separate me from the love of God, which is in Christ Jesus our Lord.

November 16

Walk - They do not know, nor do they understand; They walk about in darkness; All the foundation of the earth are unstable. Psalm 82:5 NKJV

When people are separated from God, they walk in darkness. They will continue to walk in darkness until they have been called into the light.

November 17

Praise The Lord - Oh that men would praise the LORD for his goodness, and for his wonderful works to the children of men! Psalm 107:8 KJV

We should lift our voices and praise the LORD for His wonderful works before mankind.

November 18

Grace - The grace of our Lord Jesus Christ be with you all. Amen. Philippians 4:23 KJV

As you go through your day, remember the grace of the Lord.

November 19

Blessed - Blessed are they that keep his testimonies, and that seek him with the whole heart. Psalm 119:2 KJV

Happy is a man that obeys God's Word and seeks Him with all his heart.

November 20

Upright - He stores up sound wisdom for the upright; He is a shield to those who walk uprightly; Proverbs 2:7 NKJV

If I walk upright, He stores up, He shields, He is…, He was…, He will be!!

November 21

The Word Of Christ - Let the message of Christ dwell among you richly as you teach and admonish one another with all wisdom through psalms, hymns, and songs from the Spirit, singing to God with gratitude in your hearts. Colossians 3:16 NIV

As we let the Word of Christ live within us, the Word of Christ will give us guidance on how to live and correct our mistakes.

November 22

Have Dominion - And God blessed them, and God said unto them, Be fruitful and multiply, and replenish the earth, and subdue it: and have dominion over the fish of the sea, and over the fowl of the air, and over every living thing that moveth upon the earth. Genesis 1:28 KJV

God gave man the command to replenish the earth. He gave man the authority and responsibility to manage over all the other living creatures, in the sea, in the air, and on the earth.

November 23

Walk - I say then: Walk in the Spirit, and you shall not fulfill the lust of the flesh.
Galatians 5:16 NKJV

Keep your mind on God and godly actions and conversations and say "No" to the flesh. Allow the Holy Spirit to guide your walk.

November 24

When Talking - Let your speech always be with grace, seasoned with salt, that you may know how you ought to answer each other. Colossians 4:6 NKJV

When we speak to each other, we should do it in love. We should be mindful of our tone and attitude when speaking to a group or an individual.

November 25

Peace - And the work of righteousness shall be peace; and the effect of righteousness quietness and assurance for ever. Isaiah 32:17 KJV

When the work I do is through God, I have peace in the work.

November 26

Received With Thanksgiving - For every creature of God is good, and nothing to be refused, if it be received with thanksgiving: For it is sanctified by the word of God and prayer. 1 Timothy 4:4-5 KJV

Let us give thanks for what God has made. If God made it, then it must be good as long as it is used for the purpose He intended.

November 27

Fatherless - I will not leave you orphans; I will come to you. John 14:18 NKJV

He is our heavenly Father.

November 28

Spiritual Joy - Blessed are you who hunger now, for you will be satisfied. Blessed are you who weep now, for you will laugh. Luke 6:21 NIV

You can be blessed right now with spiritual joy and be satisfied.

November 29

Walk - You shall walk in all the ways which the LORD your God has commanded you, that you may live and that it may be well with you, and that you may prolong your days in the land which you shall possess. Deuteronomy 5:33 NKJV

When God commands us to do something it is for our own good and we will be blessed when we obey. By walking in the ways of the LORD our days are prolonged.

November 30

Every Good And Perfect Gift - Every good and perfect gift is from above, coming down from the Father of the heavenly lights, who does not change like shifting shadows. James 1:17 NIV

God is pouring out blessings from heaven.

428

December 1

Peace - Behold, I will bring it health and cure, and I will cure them, and will reveal unto them the abundance of peace and truth. Jeremiah 33:6 KJV

I have peace knowing that it was truly God that healed me. When God heals you, you will not look like what you have been through.

December 2

Covenant Of Love - Know therefore that the LORD your God is God; he is the faithful God, keeping his covenant of love to a thousand generations of those who love him and keep his commandments. Deuteronomy 7:9 NIV

Faithful is our God!! The generations to come that love Him and keep His commandments will benefit from the Covenant of Love with an everlasting relationship rooted in love. I am a beneficiary of that Covenant.

December 3

Strong Tower - The name of the LORD is a strong tower: the righteous runneth into it, and is safe. Proverbs 18:10 KJV

When the storms of life are raging, I'm safe in His arms. I have everlasting safety.

December 4

Peace For Your Children - All your children will be taught by the LORD, and great will be their peace. Isaiah 54:13 NIV

There is a promise of peace for our children.

December 5

Patient In Tribulation - Rejoicing in hope; patient in tribulation; continuing instant in prayer; Romans 12:12 KJV

I will continue to pray in my afflictions as I delight in my hope.

December 6

Listen - My son, pay attention to what I say; turn your ear to my words. Do not let them out of your sight, keep them within your heart; for they are life to those who find them and health to one's whole body. Proverbs 4:20-22 NIV

One of the attributes of God is wisdom. If I take time and listen, it will lead to life and health. Listen and walk toward wisdom.

December 7

Walk - He who walks uprightly, And works righteousness, And speaks the truth in his heart; He who does not put out his money at usury, Nor does he take a bribe against the innocent. He who does these things shall never be moved. Psalm 15:2,5 NKJV

He who does these things will be planted on a solid foundation. Walk-in this way!!

December 8

All Scripture - All scripture is given by inspiration of God, and is profitable for doctrine, for reproof, for correction, for instruction in righteousness: 2 Timothy 3:16 KJV

All Scriptures are inspired by God, to teach me how to walk the Scripture out by rebuking, correcting and training me in righteousness.

December 9

I Shall Not Be Moved - I have set the LORD always before me: because he is at my right hand, I shall not be moved. Psalm 16:8 KJV

When my eyes are focused on the LORD, I will not be distracted.

December 10

Mercy On The Afflicted - Sing, O heavens! Be joyful, O earth! And break out in singing, O mountains! For the LORD has comforted His people, And will have mercy on His afflicted. Isaiah 49:13 NKJV

I will praise you O LORD with my whole heart. I
know you will comfort me and have mercy on me.

December 11

Transformed - And do not be conformed to this world, but be transformed by the renewing of your mind, that you may prove what is that good and acceptable and perfect will of God. Romans 12:2 NKJV

As God changes the way I think, I will learn to know His will for me.

December 12

Stand - Now therefore stand and see this great thing, which the LORD will do before your eyes. 1 Samuel 12:16 KJV

I will stand and see the victory of the Lord before my eyes.

December 13

He Satisfies - For he satifieth the longing soul, and filleth the hungry soul with goodness. Psalm 107:9 KJV

Only God can satisfy this yearning desire deep in my soul with goodness. As I grow closer to Him, I thirst and hunger for His righteousness.

December 14

Walk - When you walk, your steps will not be hindered, And when you run, you will not stumble.
Proverbs 4:12 NKJV

Keep your feet on the path of righteousness and your walking and running will not be hindered.

December 15

Your Enemy - On the contrary: "If your enemy is hungry, feed him; if he is thirsty, give him something to drink. In doing this, you will heap burning coals on his head." Do not be overcome by evil, but overcome evil with good. Romans 12:20-21 NIV

Help me to see my enemies' needs and offer help. My kindness might lead them to regret their actions. With your help, when evil is offered to me, I will offer kindness that others may see You in me.

December 16

The Gospel - And he said unto them, Go ye into all the world, and preach the gospel to every creature. Mark 16:15 KJV

I have been commissioned to go and spread the gospel to everyone.

December 17

I Will Sing - But I will sing of your strength, in the morning I will sing of your love; for you are my fortress, my refuge in times of trouble. Psalm 59:16 NIV

You continue to show me Your love and strength. I will sing praises to You for You are my shield in the time of trouble.

December 18

Pray - And when you pray, do not use vain repetitions as the heathen do. For they think that they will be heard for their many words. Matthew 6:7 NKJV

Help me to pray with faith, assuring that my prayer will be answered and not for a show with empty words.

December 19

My Portion - The LORD is my portion, saith my soul; therefore will I hope in him. Lamentations 3:24 KJV

Material things and man can only fill the hole(s) in my life temporarily. God alone can provide for me infinitely. My hope is in Him and He is my portion.

December 20

Jehovahjireh - Abraham looked up and there in the thicket he saw a ram caught by its horns. He went over and took the ram and sacrificed it as a burnt offering instead of his son. So Abraham called that place The Lord Will Provide. And to this day it is said, "On the mountain of the LORD it will be provided." Genesis 22:13-14 NIV

I will obey God and He will provide all of my needs. He is an on-time God.

December 21

Walk - Teach me Your way, O LORD: I will walk in Your truth; Unite my heart to fear Your name. Psalm 86:11 NKJV

Teach me Your Word so that the path I walk is walking in Your truth. Keep my heart focused on You.

602

December 22

Mercies - It is of the LORD's mercies that we are not consumed, because his compassions fail not. They are new every morning; great is thy faithfulness. Lamentations 3:22-23 KJV

I can never use up all of God's mercies. I am given new mercies each morning. I wake up with mercies to get me through that day and the day after and the day after. His mercies will never come to an end.

December 23

Removed Transgressions - As far as the east is from the west, So far has He removed our transgressions from us. Psalm 103:12 NKJV

Our sins have been removed so far from us that the distance is immeasurable. Hallelujah!!

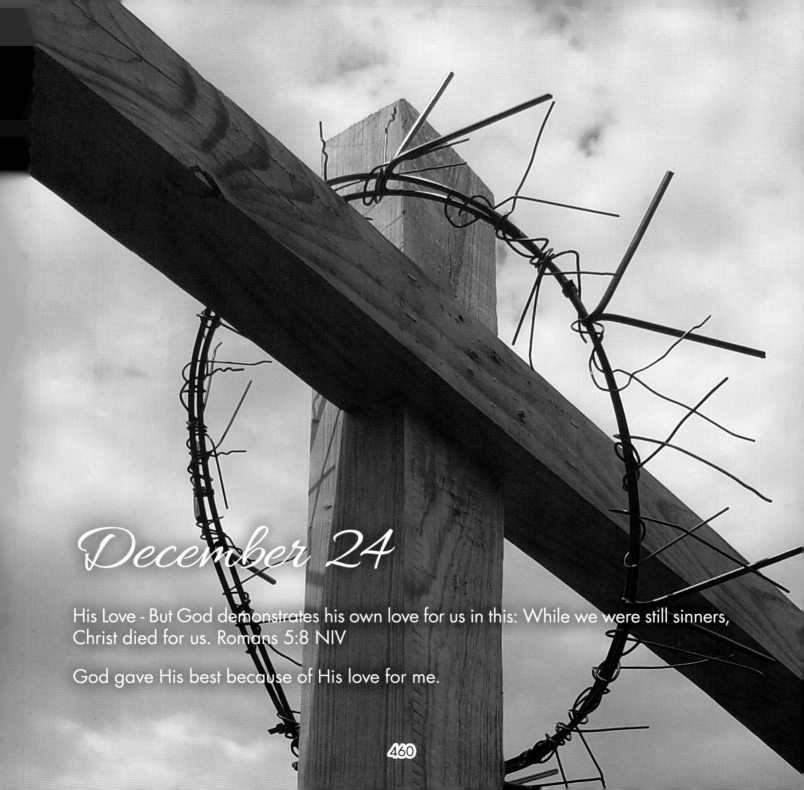

December 24

His Love - But God demonstrates his own love for us in this: While we were still sinners, Christ died for us. Romans 5:8 NIV

God gave His best because of His love for me.

December 25

Prince OF Peace - For unto us a child is born, unto us a son is given: and the government shall be upon his shoulder: and his name shall be called Wonderful, Counselor, The mighty God, The everlasting Father, The Prince of Peace. Isaiah 9:6 KJV

This is the prophecy about the coming Messiah.
He will be called many names. He is The Prince
of Peace.

December 26

His Will - Now may the God of peace who brought up our Lord Jesus from the dead, that great Shepherd of the sheep, through the blood of everlasting covenant, make you complete in every good work to do His will, working in you what is well pleasing in His sight, through Jesus Christ, to whom be glory forever and ever. Amen. Hebrews 13:20-21 NKJV

I speak blessings over your day, month and year.
Do the good work you have been destined to do,
in the name of Jesus. Amen.

December 27

He calms - He calms the storm, So that its waves are still. Psalm 107:29 NKJV

Calmness comes from our omnipotent God and Him alone.

December 28

Walk - For we walk by faith, and not by sight. 2 Corinthians 5:7 NKJV

My walk is in the hope I have in You Lord. I may be blinded or mislead by what I see.

December 29

Strength And Refuge - God is our refuge and strength, a very present help in trouble. Psalm 46:1 KJV

At any time, any place or under any situation God is my shelter and power.

December 30

Mercy - O give thanks unto the LORD; for he is good: because his mercy endureth for ever. Psalm 118:1 KJV

I thank the LORD for His mercies that are new every morning and for His mercies on tomorrow and for His mercies on the day after tomorrow and forevermore.

December 31

Every Knee Shall Bow - That at the name of Jesus every knee should bow, of things in heaven, and things in earth, and things under the earth; And that every one shall confess that Jesus Christ is Lord, to the glory of God the Father. Philippians 2:10-11 KJV

In His name, all creation will bow and acknowledge that He is Lord. I thank God, I have accepted His gift of salvation. If you have not accepted Jesus as your Lord and Savior, you can accept Him now. If you declare with your mouth "Jesus is Lord," and believe in your heart that God raised him from the dead, you will be saved. Romans 10:9 NIV.

Photo Credits

Cover page photo taken at MYRIAD BOTANICAL GARDENS, OKLAHOMA CITY, OK.; by Rchard C. Washington II; Creative Director of Vision93.com

January

1 Linda Reynolds; 2 Patricia Emerson; 3 Patricia Emerson; 4 Linda Reynolds; 5 Tricia Voigt; 6 Tom Sledge; 7 William Mullendore; 8 Laura Beth Winstead; 9 Laura Beth Winstead; 10 Laura Beth Winstead; 11 Caryn Miller; 12 Chandra Welt; 13 Tom Sledge; 14 Linda Reynolds; 15 Rick Washington; 16 Rick Washington; 17 Amanda Drake; 18 Patricia Emerson; 19 Patricia Emerson; 20 Tom Sledge; 21 Linda Reynolds; 22 Chandra Welt; 23 Chandra Welt; 24 Rick Washington; 25 Lisa Ramirez; 26 Lisa Ramirez; 27 Tom Sledge; 28 Amanda Drake; 29 Laura Beth Winstead; 30 Laura Beth Winstead; 31 Debra Kramer.

February

1 Cecilyn Washington; 2 Richard Washington; 3 William Mullendore; 4 Richard Washington; 5 Cecilyn Washington; 6 Richard Washington; 7 Cecilyn Washington; 8 Gina Herndon; 9 Rick Washington; 10 Rick Washington; 11 Phatsany Nakhalath; 12 Richard Washington; 13 Marques Thomas; 14 Phatsany Nakhalath; 15 Mark Dominguez; 16 Amanda Drake; 17 Richard Washington; 18 Linda Reynolds; 19 Cecilyn Washington; 20 Richard Washington; 21 Richard Washington; 22 Cecilyn Washington; 23 Richard Washington; 24 Cecilyn Washington; 25 Amanda Drake; 26 Clara Psikal; 27 Clara Psikal; 28 Gina Herndon; 29 Richard Washington.

March

1 Richard Washington; 2 Caryn Miller; 3 Gina Herndon; 4 Linda Reynolds; 5 Rick Washington; 6 Rick Washington; 7 Richard Washington; 8 Sharon Thomas; 9 Evelyn Dooley; 10 Tom Sledge; 11 Adam Paty; 12 Adam Paty; 13 Laura Beth Winstead; 14 Laura Beth Winstead; 15 Cecilyn Washington; 16 Tom Sledge; 17 Richard Washington; 18 Rick Washington; 19 Rick Washington; 20 Richard Washington; 21 Richard Washington; 22 Richard Washington; 23 Cecilyn Washington; 24 Cecilyn Washington; 25 Richard Washington; 26 Richard Washington; 27 Sharon Thomas; 28 Sharon Thomas; 29 Adam Paty; 30 Sharon Thomas; 31 Sharon Thomas.

April

1 Richard Washington; 2 Richard Washington MYRIAD BOTANICAL GARDENS, OKLAHOMA CITY, OK.; 3 Richard Washington MYRIAD BOTANICAL GARDENS, OKLAHOMA CITY, OK.; 4 Cecilyn Washington; 5 Richard Washington; 6 Richard Washington; 7 Cecilyn Washington; 8 William Mullendore; 9 William Mullendore; 10 William Mullendore; 11 Adam Paty; 12 Richard Washington MYRIAD BOTANICAL GARDENS, OKLAHOMA CITY, OK.; 13 Cecilyn Washington; 14 William Mullendore; 15 Ladonna Rogers; 16 Cindy Gouge; 17 Tricia Voigt; 18 Richard Washington; 19 Rick Washington; 20 Sharon Thomas; 21 Amber Louis; 22 Sharon Thomas; 23 Richard Washington; 24 Richard Washington MYRIAD BOTANICAL GARDENS, OKLAHOMA CITY, OK.; 25 Richard Washington; 26 Cecilyn Washington; 27 Richard Washington; 28 Cecilyn Washington; 29 Cecilyn Washington; 30 Heath Wiederstein.

May

Amanda Robinson, But God!!; 1 Sylvia Bridges; 2 Cecilyn Washington; 3 Cecilyn Washington; 4 Richard Washington; 5 Cecilyn Washington; 6 Linda Reynolds; 7 Richard Washington; 8 Richard Washington MYRIAD BOTANICAL GARDENS, OKLAHOMA CITY, OK.; 9 Richard Washington; 10 Cecilyn Washington; 11 Cindy Gouge; 12 Phatsany Nakhalath; 13 Richard Washington; 14 Cecilyn Washington; 15 Laura Beth Winstead; 16 Richard Washington MYRIAD BOTANICAL GARDENS, OKLAHOMA CITY, OK.; 17 Chandra Welt; 18 Richard Washington; 19 Richard Washington; 20 Amanda Robinson; 21 Richard Washington; 22 Richard Washington MYRIAD BOTANICAL GARDENS, OKLAHOMA CITY, OK.; 23 Sharon Thomas; 24 Richard Washington MYRIAD BOTANICAL GARDENS, OKLAHOMA CITY, OK.; 25 William Mullendore; 26 Adam Paty; 27 Sylvia Bridges; 28 Mark Dominguez; 29 Richard Washington; 30 Laura Beth Winstead; 31 Sherry Thompson.

June

1 Richard Washington; 2 Cecilyn Washington; 3 Cecilyn Washington; 4 Adam Paty; 5 Adam Paty; 6 Adam Paty; 7 Richard Washington; 8 Richard Washington; 9 Richard Washington MYRIAD BOTANICAL GARDENS, OKLAHOMA CITY, OK.; 10 Cecilyn Washington; 11 Richard Washington MYRIAD BOTANICAL GARDENS, OKLAHOMA CITY, OK.; 12 Cecilyn Washington; 13 Richard Washington; 14 Richard Washington MYRIAD BOTANICAL GARDENS, OKLAHOMA CITY, OK.; 15 Tom Sledge; 16 Chandra Welt; 17 Rick Washington; 18 Linda Reynolds; 19 Laura Beth Winstead; 20 Richard Washington; 21 Richard Washington; 22 Erica Kinsey; 23 Erica Kinsey; 24 Caryn Miller; 25 Caryn Miller; 26 Cecilyn Washington; 27 Sharon Thomas; 28 Adam Paty; 29 Sharon Thomas; 30 Richard Washington MYRIAD BOTANICAL GARDENS, OKLAHOMA CITY, OK.

July

1 Marques Thomas; 2 Marques Thomas; 3 Mark Dominguez; 4 Cecilyn Washington; 5 Kelly Swiney; 6 Sharon Thomas; 7 Tom Sledge; 8 Analysha Ramirez; 9 Richard Washington; 10 Richard Washington; 11 Richard Washington; 12 Tricia Voigt; 13 Cindy Gouge; 14 Debra Kramer; 15 Debra Kramer; 16 Traci Ford; 17 Traci Ford; 18 Richard Washington; 19 Rick Washington; 20 Sharon Thomas; 21 LaDonna Rogers; 22 Richard Washington; 23 Marquel Wright; 24 Richard Washington; 25 Cecilyn Washington; 26 Sara Troyer; 27 Sharon Thomas; 28 Cecilyn Washington; 29 Pamela Gaines; 30 Richard Washington; 31 Laura Beth Winstead.

August

1 Amanda Drake; 2 Danielle Damiano; 3 Sharon Thomas; 4 Sherry Thompson; 5 Marsha Murphy; 6 Charles Thuo; 7 Charles Thuo; 8 Laura Beth Winstead; 9 Clara Psikal; 10 Sharon Thomas; 11 Cecilyn Washington; 12 Cecilyn Washington; 13 Cecilyn Washington; 14 Danielle Damiano; 15 Diane Ford; 16 Gina Herndon; 17 Tom Sledge; 18 Unknown; 19 Danielle Damiano; 20 Donna Huddleston; 21 Cecilyn Washington; 22 Heath Wiederstein; 23 Amanda Robinson; 24 Diane Ford; 25 Adam Paty; 26 Phatsany Nakhalath; 27 Phatsany Nakhalath; 28 Sharon Thomas; 29 William Mullendore; 30 JaKara Washington; 31 Richard Washington.

September

Heath Wiederstein, To God be the Glory!!; 1 Richard Washington; 2 Gina Herndon; 3 Clara Psikal; 4 Laura Beth Winstead; 5 Clara Psikal; 6 Richard Washington; 7 Richard Washington; 8 Laura Beth Winstead; 9 Cecilyn Washington; 10 Rick Washington; 11 Cecilyn Washington; 12 Richard Washington MYRIAD BOTANICAL GARDENS, OKLAHOMA CITY, OK.; 13 Richard Washington MYRIAD BOTANICAL GARDENS, OKLAHOMA CITY, OK.; 14 Cecilyn Washington; 15 Elda Ochoa; 16 Tom Sledge; 17 Amber Louis; 18 Adam Paty; 19 Adam Paty; 20 Richard Washington MYRIAD BOTANICAL GARDENS, OKLAHOMA CITY, OK.; 21 Richard Washington; 22 Adam Paty; 23 Richard Washington; 24 Phatsany Nakhalath; 25 Tyrone Galbreath; 26 Tyrone Galbreath; 27 Richard Washington; 28   Cecilyn Washington; 29 Richard Washington; 30 Heath Wiederstein.

October

1 Gina Herndon; 2 Adam Paty; 3 Adam Paty; 4 Richard Washington MYRIAD BOTANICAL GARDENS, OKLAHOMA CITY, OK.; 5 Richard Washington; 6 Cecilyn Washington; 7 Cecilyn Washington; 8 Chandra Welt; 9 Chandra Welt; 10 JaKara Washington; 11 Caryn Miller; 12 Richard Washington; 13 Richard Washington; 14 Tom Sledge; 15 Hollie Teter; 16 Richard Washington; 17 Laura Beth Winstead; 18 William Mullendore; 19 William Mullendore; 20 William Mullendore; 21 Richard Washington; 22 Richard Washington; 23 Richard Washington MYRIAD BOTANICAL GARDENS, OKLAHOMA CITY, OK.; 24 Richard Washington; 25 Adam Paty; 26 Adam Paty; 27 Tom Sledge; 28 Tom Sledge; 29 Richard Washington; 30 Laura Beth Winstead; 31 Laura Beth Winstead.

November

1 Richard Washington MYRIAD BOTANICAL GARDENS, OKLAHOMA CITY, OK.; 2 Richard Washington; 3 William Mullendore; 4 Cecilyn Washington; 5 Cecilyn Washington; 6 Caryn Miller; 7 Caryn Miller; 8 Rick Washington; 9 Adam Paty; 10 Linda Reynolds; 11 Linda Reynolds; 12 Gina Herndon; 13 Lynn Finley; 14 William Mullendore; 15 William Mullendore; 16 Adam Paty; 17 Adam Paty; 18 Unknown; 19 Unknown; 20 Rick Washington; 21 Linda Reynolds; 22 Cecilyn Washington; 23 Cecilyn Washington; 24 Cecilyn Washington; 25 Cecilyn Washington; 26 Richard Washington; 27 Chandra Welt; 28 Chandra Welt; 29 Adam Paty; 30 Linda Reynolds

December

1 Danielle Damiano; 2 Linda Reynolds; 3 Cecilyn Washington; 4 Kenysha Mumford; 5 Laura Beth Winstead; 6 Erica Kinsey; 7 Linda Reynolds; 8 Caryn Miller; 9 Rick Washington; 10 Linda Reynolds; 11 Chandra Welt; 12 Chandra Welt; 13 Cecilyn Washington; 14 Richard Washington MYRIAD BOTANICAL GARDENS, OKLAHOMA CITY, OK.; 15 Richard Washington; 16 Cecilyn Washington; 17 Amber Louis; 18 William Mullendore; 19 Richard Washington; 20 Cecilyn Washington; 21 Cecilyn Washington; 22 Cecilyn Washington; 23 Cecilyn Washington; 24 Cecilyn Washington; 25 Patricia Emerson; 26 Adam Paty; 27 William Mullendore; 28 Gina Herndon; 29 Gina Herndon; 30 Amanda Drake; 31 Terri Waldman.